HAMPSTEAD PAST

First published 1989
by Historical Publications Ltd.
54 Station Road, New Barnet, Herts
and 32 Ellington Street, London, N7 8PL
(Telephone 01–607 1628)

Reprinted 1997

ISBN 0 948667 05 2

Typeset by Historical Publications Ltd
and Fakenham Photosetting, Fakenham.

Printed and bound in Great Britain by
Butler & Tanner Ltd, Frome and London

HAMPSTEAD PAST

A Visual History
of Hampstead

by
Christopher Wade

HISTORICAL PUBLICATIONS

The Illustrations

The following have kindly allowed the publication of illustrations:

London Borough of Camden, Local History Library: 7, 10, 14, 19, 20, 21, 26, 31, 35, 41, 42, 45, 49, 50, 51, 53, 57, 58, 64, 66, 67, 68, 73, 75, 76, 78, 91, 92, 95, 101, 107, 114, 115, 116, 119, 120, 121, 122, 124, 126, 127, 135, 138, 141, 142, 143, 144, 145, 146, 147, 148, 149, 150, 151, 152, 154, 155, 156, 161, 164, 168, 170,174, 175, 176, 177, 178, 182, 184, 185, 186, 187, 190, 192, 194.
Roger Cline 18.
The Hugh Curtis Collection, 44, 60, 61, 83, 102, 133, 139.
Alan Farmer, 1, 17, 104, 112.
Greater London Record Office 46, 117, 129, 189, 191.
M.J. Hammerson 90, 106, 123.
Hampstead Museum: 8, 11, 39, 40, 43, 47, 54, 55, 56, 62, 65, 77, 81, 84, 98, 99, 105, 110, 130, 134, 140, 153, 157, 167, 171, 173, 179, 180, 183, 193.
National Monuments Record 132, 160, 163.
South Hampstead High School 131.
Christopher Wade 136, 166, 169, 172.
Westfield College 158.
Other illustrations are from the collection of *Historical Publications Ltd*.

The cover illustration of Heath Street by P.L. Forbes, 1900 is reproduced by kind permission of the London Borough of Camden.

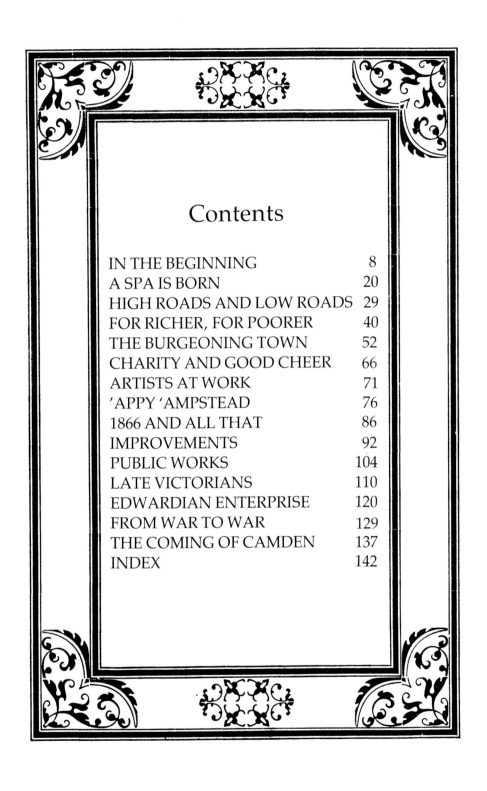

Contents

IN THE BEGINNING   8
A SPA IS BORN   20
HIGH ROADS AND LOW ROADS   29
FOR RICHER, FOR POORER   40
THE BURGEONING TOWN   52
CHARITY AND GOOD CHEER   66
ARTISTS AT WORK   71
'APPY 'AMPSTEAD   76
1866 AND ALL THAT   86
IMPROVEMENTS   92
PUBLIC WORKS   104
LATE VICTORIANS   110
EDWARDIAN ENTERPRISE   120
FROM WAR TO WAR   129
THE COMING OF CAMDEN   137
INDEX   142

Acknowledgements

Much of the information in this book derives from the Camden History Society's surveys, *The Streets of Hampstead*, in which I was heavily involved. Those publications were themselves indebted to the two early Hampstead histories, *The Topography and Natural History of Hampstead* by J.J. Park (1814), and *The Annals of Hampstead* by Thomas J. Barratt (1912). Since then F.M.L. Thompson's *Hampstead, Building a Borough* (1974) and John Richardson's millennium celebration, *Hampstead One Thousand* (1986) have proved useful.

Thanks are due also to other publications from the Camden History Society, including individual research by its members, too numerous to mention. Other helpful sources have been two books on Hampstead Heath by C.W. Ikin (1971, revised 1985), and by Alan Farmer (1984), and over a century of weekly editions of the *Hampstead and Highgate Express*.

For illustrations, help came again from Barratt, from the Hampstead Museum at Burgh House, and especially from *Images of Hampstead* by Jenkins, Ditchburn and George, published in 1982.

But, as ever, the main source of material was Camden's Local History Library at Swiss Cottage, where the librarian Malcolm Holmes and his staff provided steady support as did, in many other directions, my wife, Diana.

Introduction

As a pictorial history of Hampstead, this book can only reflect a few of the pleasures and curiosities of this beguiling place. The recorded history of the area goes back over a thousand years, embracing Anglo-Saxon charters, the Domesday Book, medieval manuscripts and many later documents, but it is not until the 18th century and the heyday of Hampstead Spa that the first topographical prints begin to emerge in any quantity. After that there are pictures in profusion, and it has to be said that most of these views appear so romanticised that, at first, we do not know how much to believe. The primary purpose of a print, after all, was to be so picturesque that it would richly reward its publisher.

Even so, view upon view shows Hampstead as a charming rural retreat, an elegant Georgian town, or later a bosky Victorian suburb and, as we are quite certain that Hampstead today *is* an attractive and individual locality, so must we believe in most of the fairness and quaintness of Hampstead's past.

This selection of pictures illustrates many facets of Hampstead down the ages – from the village in Middlesex to the 'village' in Camden. But here also is the Hampstead beloved of artists and writers, the country mansions, the famous pubs, the popular Heath and especially 'Appy 'Ampstead, the playground of Londoners on holiday.

The Spa turned Hampstead into a health resort, and the consequent crowds of visitors turned it into a pleasure resort: it has stayed that way ever since.

Christopher Wade
May 1989

1. *View of Hampstead from Primrose Hill* by John Royce, 1775.

In the Beginning

ASPIRATIONS

The story of Hampstead's development over the centuries is dominated by three recurring aspirations – its hill, its heath and its healthiness.

The hill of Hampstead, rising rapidly from Chalk Farm or Kilburn to its peak at Jack Straw's Castle, is part of the ridge that stretches to Highgate, usually known as the Northern Heights of London. This wrinkle in time, left behind by the Ice Age, became a desirable hilltop for mesolithic man, for bronze age settlers and for medieval farmers. The Domesday Book shows Hamestede, the Anglo-Saxon for homestead, as a small farm with pigs and ploughs, all valued at fifty shillings. Later the village sprouted two windmills, and these appear in one of the earliest views of our hill, a panorama of London by Visscher. Even as late as 1775, the view of Hampstead from Primrose Hill *(1)* is of a rural community perched precariously on its lofty height.

Hampstead remained aloof from the city until the middle of the last century, when the tide of building swept up the hill. With the smogs and crowds and hurly-burly in lower London, a home on the heights of Hampstead became more and more covetable and,

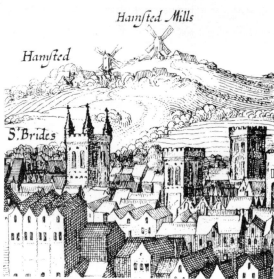

2. The heights of Hampstead and its two windmills are shown in this detail from Visscher's *View of London*, published before 1632.

with the uphill problems of transport and servicing industries, more and more expensive. Much of Hampstead's very special and superior flavour today, and perhaps its high-mindedness, comes first from its enviable and luxurious location.

The Ice Age can also be credited with Hampstead Heath, the largest stretch of countryside in any city in the world. The Heath is here largely because the

3. Hampstead Heath: Branch Hill Pond by John Constable, 1821, a view from the West Heath towards the West End of Hampstead.

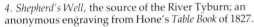

4. Shepherd's Well, the source of the River Tyburn; an anonymous engraving from Hone's *Table Book* of 1827.

crest of the hill is covered by sand and gravel, on which no richer crops would grow. For centuries this was known as 'the Common', partly covered by heather and gorse, and partly used as grazing land.

The healthiness of Hampstead followed naturally from the hill and the Heath. Apart from the fresh country air at 440ft above sea level, there was the wonderful water. Some of this was of medicinal interest, and brought about the Spa in Well Walk, but the most important spring was at Shepherd's Well. This is still marked by a fountain at the junction of Fitzjohns Avenue and Akenside Road: it disappeared when the avenue was built in the 1870s. Here the water was so pure that it never froze, and villagers would visit it with their buckets at all times of the year. For the idle rich, there were water-carriers who would deliver to the door for one penny per bucket. The spring was also the source of the River Tyburn, which filled the lakes of Regent's Park and Buckingham Palace, as well as passing near the gallows at Marble Arch, the famous Tyburn Tree.

Three other rivers, the Westbourne, the Brent and the Fleet, rise in Hampstead but, like the Tyburn, have largely become 'lost' or gone below. At the least, the beginnings of the Fleet can be seen on the Heath, filling all the ponds before crossing Fleet Road and heading for Fleet Street.

The quantity and purity of water in Hampstead created many a healthy laundry business around the Heath. Colonies of washerwomen made a living here because their far-flung customers found that Hampstead gave the whitest wash. The bushes of the Heath were often to be found festooned with washing, hung out to dry, and a skipper on the Thames once remarked that it looked as if the hill of Hampstead was capped with snow.

CLERICS

The recorded history of Hampstead begins with the Anglo-Saxon charters, which put the manor of Hampstead into ecclesiastical hands. In the best-known document of AD986, held by the British Library, King Ethelred the Unready granted Hampstead to the monastery of St Peter's, Westminster.

The first documentary evidence of a place of worship in central Hampstead comes in 1312, but the medieval parish church of Hampstead is shown in an old engraving *(6)* to date back to the previous century at the latest. The picture tells the story. Among the conglomeration of assorted styles and periods is a romanesque two-light east window that suggests a date of about 1220–40. The stone and timber structure, with its typical Middlesex bellcote, had its main entrance under a two-storey south porch and, unlike the present parish church on the same site, it was dedicated to the Blessed Virgin Mary and had its altar

at the east end.

By 1710, this rambling building was found too small and dilapidated for Hampstead's larger and smarter population. The parishioners petitioned Parliament for a new church, stressing that 'the inhabitants could not attend Divine Worship without apparent hazard to their lives'. They had to wait 37 years for results.

On the western borders of the parish Kilburn Priory originated as a hermit cell in the twelfth cen-

5. *Remains of Kilburn Priory, as it appeared in 1722*, an etching by J. Quilley.

6. *View of the Old Church at Hampstead*, drawn by John Goldar and published in 1785: this was forty years after the building was demolished to make way for the present parish church.

tury. Standing on the banks of a stream, the Kyle Bourn (meaning cold water), and alongside the Roman Watling Street (now transformed into Kilburn High Road), the Priory was well placed to offer refreshment to pilgrims on the road to the shrine of St Alban. In fact by the fifteenth century, the few resident nuns were so overwhelmed by demands for hospitality that they had to beg for help from the Abbot of Westminster. The Priory was closed by the Dissolution of the Monasteries under Henry VIII: it crumbled and disappeared. But railway works in the 1850s unearthed some foundations and human remains, and in 1877 a fragment of ornamental brass was found. This tiny memorial, only three inches high, and dated about 1390, can now be seen in St Mary's, Abbey Road, and is our only locally surviving souvenir of the Priory and of medieval Hampstead.

TUDORS

Tudor monarchs had reason to look kindly on Hampstead. Some of them are known to have sent the palace laundry for a superior wash in Hampstead's streams, and others encouraged the use of those streams to improve London's water supply. The Heath ponds were, in fact, formed in Tudor times.

Henry VIII not only acquired valuable local estates from Westminster Abbey at the Dissolution, but much enjoyed hunting on the Heath and, in 1545, issued a proclamation reserving all hare, partridge, pheasant and heron for himself. Anyone caught poaching on the Heath would be 'punished at His Majesty's will and pleasure'.

The king's hunting doubtless took him to the northern borders of Hampstead and a 340-acre estate at North End called Wyldes, owned by the Leper Hospital of St James, which was itself in the custody of Eton College. In 1531 Henry dissolved the hospital, on which site he built St James's Palace, but he allowed the College to keep Wyldes, as well as its other Hampstead property at Chalcots (now the Eton Estate at Chalk Farm). The farmland has been converted to the Hampstead Heath Extension and parts of Hampstead Garden Suburb, but the early 17th-century farmhouse and its barn have survived as two picturesque dwellings. Both bear plaques to past residents – one to the artist, John Linnell, and his mystic friend, William Blake, the other to Sir Raymond Unwin, chief architect of the Garden Suburb. One distinguished lodger here not commemorated was Charles Dickens, who came to Wyldes in 1837 to mourn the death of his sister-in-law, Mary Hogarth: he knew North End well enough to include

7. Wyldes Farm, 1830, from a watercolour by George Barnard.

8. *The flagstaff* by Whitestone Pond, an undated sketch by George du Maurier, featuring his dog and one of his daughters.

it in Bill Sykes' flight path in *Oliver Twist*.

The hill of Hampstead was helpful to Elizabeth I in 1588, when a chain of beacons was needed to warn her citizens of the approaching Armada and a possible Spanish invasion. The beacon stood on the site of the present flagstaff by Whitestone Pond and communicated with a similar fire signal near Harrow. 'From Surrey's pleasant hills,' wrote Lord Macaulay in his *Lay of the Spanish Armada*, 'flew those bright couriers forth. High on bleak Hampstead's swarthy moor, they started for the north.' Harrow is no longer visible from the flagstaff and, when a celebratory beacon chain was lit in 1988, Hampstead's bonfire was on Parliament Hill.

Elizabeth included Hampstead in a royal progress in 1593, perhaps arranged by her Chief Clerk of the Privy Council, William Waad, who lived at Belsize House. Sir William inherited his palace appointment and his grand house from his father, Armigal Waad, who had been Clerk of the Council to Henry VIII and Edward VI. Armigal had earlier been a merchant adventurer, whose voyages to America around 1540 had earned him the sobriquet 'the English Columbus'. He died at Belsize in 1568 and was buried in the chancel of the parish church, but his 'fine alabaster monument' has gone. Sir William continued as Clerk of the Council to James I, who knighted him, and he was a commissioner at the trials of Sir Walter Raleigh and Guy Fawkes. He died at Belsize in 1623.

Belsize, a name derived from the French *bel assis*, meaning 'beautifully situated', was a subdivision of the manor of Hampstead. Its earliest mention was in 1317, in the will of Sir Roger le Brabazon, Lord Chief Justice to Edward II: he left this 'messuage and fifty-seven acres of land' to Westminster Abbey. The messuage was Belsize House which, after the Dissolution, passed to the new Bishop of Westminster, who

9. *Sir William Waad*, court official and Lord of Belsize; from an old engraving.

leased it to the Waad family for a yearly rent of £19 and ten loads each of hay and oats. Lord Wotton inherited and improved the property in the 1660s, so much so that it attracted visits from two noted diarists. Samuel Pepys praised the gardens with their 'brave orange and lemon trees', but John Evelyn found them 'ill kept' and decried the soil, as have many gardeners later, for being 'cold weeping clay'.

Just north of this mansion (whose later history is dealt with in the section called A SPA IS BORN *(pages 20–28)*, about half-way down Belsize Lane, was the farmhouse of the manor farm. As the lane was on private land the farmer charged a penny toll to any passing vehicle, and often left his daughter in charge of the toll-gate. According to local tradition she was in charge one day when Queen Victoria drove up in her carriage on her way to visit Rosslyn House. The girl was not that impressed and successfully demanded her penny toll.

STUARTS

Yet another royal patron of Hampstead was James I, who stayed at the curiously-named Chicken House on the upper eastern slope of Rosslyn Hill on 25 August 1619. We know this exact date from the in-

10. *Belsize Farm* and tollhouse in Belsize Lane, 1859, from a watercolour by G. Maund.

11. *The Chicken House* in Rosslyn Hill, an engraving of 1797
by J.P. Malcolm.

12. The window in the Chicken House, recording the visit of James I and the Duke of Buckingham; an engraving by W.P. Sherlock, published in 1814.

scription on a stained glass window in the house, which made a pictorial record of the visit of the king and his favourite, the Duke of Buckingham.

The Chicken House was then probably a newly-built hunting lodge, but by the 1750s it had become a tavern and later a lodging house, whose occupants included William Murray, the future Lord Mansfield. In the 1880s, when it was demolished, the house was locally described as a den of thieves. The fate of the historic window remains a mystery. It was salvaged from the house by a rich merchant, Sir Thomas Neave of Branch Hill Lodge, who added it to his collection. But recent enquiries about it among his descendants have drawn a blank.

James I is distantly associated with another Hampstead location – the King of Bohemia in the High Street, probably named after James's popular son-in-law. This is certainly the oldest pub name in Hampstead and, though its first mention is 1680, its origins are doubtless earlier.

Nearly opposite the Chicken House in Rosslyn Hill was a more stately home called Vane House. This was built in the mid-17th century by the brilliant statesman, Harry Vane, who had become Governor of Massachusetts by the age of twenty-four, and an

13. Sir Harry Vane (1612–62), from an engraving published by S. Woodburn in 1811.

14. *The King of Bohemia* in the High Street, from a watercolour by Harold Lawes, 1886.

15. *House built and inhabited by Sir Henry Vane at Hampstead*, 1813, drawn by William Davison.

16. *The Hollow Elm of Hampstead*, drawn and engraved by Wenceslaus Hollar in 1653.

MP, civil servant and knight by twenty-seven. But his sympathies wavered between the king and the Commonwealth, so much so that he was nicknamed 'the prince of paradoxes' and 'Sir Harry Weathervane'. He enthusiastically championed the policies of Cromwell until the execution of Charles I, when he accused his friend of tyranny.'The Lord deliver me from Sir Harry Vane,' once cried the Protector, who is said to have visited Vane House along with Milton and Marvell.

After Charles II was restored to the throne, Sir Harry retired to his Hampstead home and reputedly had underground passages dug for emergency escape. But the royal troops arrived and marched him down to the Tower of London.' He is too dangerous a man to let live,' said the king, 'if we can honestly put him out of the way', and Vane was tried and executed for treason in 1662. His name is perpetuated in a housing development on the site and on a plaque erected in 1897 on his gatepost, the only sur-

viving remnant of his once noble estate.

In the 1740s the house was occupied by the influential theologian, Bishop Butler and, after the Crimean War, the few remaining buildings were incorporated into the Royal Soldiers' Daughters Home. The house was finally demolished in 1970 and the Daughters moved to a modern block.

One of Hampstead's earliest sideshows, which attracted much curiosity and custom in the 1650s, was the great Hollow Elm. Standing somewhere near the brow of the hill, this tree had been fitted out with a spiral staircase inside the trunk, with forty-two steps and sixteen openings. At the top, thirty-three feet above the ground, was an octagonal turret, which would hold six sitting and fourteen standing, and an enterprising tutor even began a school up there for twelve young gentlemen. Thomas Barratt in his monumental *Annals of Hampstead*, not noted for its witticisms, commented that this 'gave Hampstead a start in Higher Education'. At the foot of the tree

17. *Upper Terrace Avenue*, now known as Judges Walk, drawn by George Stanfield, *c*1850.

was pinned *A Welcome*:

> Civil people, you welcome be
> That come to view this Hollow Tree
> Debaucht Drunkard, Ranting Whore,
> Come no such within this Dore:
> Wanton Boys and ranting Rigs,
> Cut no Bowes and break no Sprigs.

Greater poets of the day, such as Robert Codrington, were ecstatic about the view from the top:

> (Not just) smooth Richmond's streams not Acton's mill,
> Nor Windsor's castle, nor yet Shooter's Hill...
> But a swift view, which most delightful shows,
> And doth them all, and all at once, inclose.

And at least one poet noted that the pleasures of the neighbourhood included a Well, the first suggestion that Hampstead might one day become a Spa.

The healthiness of Hampstead was in much demand during the plague years in the City of London. There is no truth in the oft-quoted story that citizens took refuge in the Vale of Health, for it was itself an unhealthy swamp until it was drained in 1777. But there is some evidence that the judiciary came up to Hampstead in the 1660s and held their assizes on the edge of the Heath. It may be the reason for the name Judges Walk, the avenue of trees overlooking the West Heath, though the name was introduced officially only earlier this century. At the same time, the traditional explanation was verified by none less than Sir Francis Palgrave in the 1850s, who based it on 'an old law book'.

There were other reasons for coming to Hampstead in the late 17th century, apart from the healthy air and water and the wonders of nature. Protestant dissenters, who could preach only beyond a five mile radius from Charing Cross, found sympathy in Hampstead and a group of them registered their meeting place on Rosslyn Hill in 1691. Religious worship has continued on or near this site for almost three hundred years, currently in the Unitarian Chapel on Rosslyn Hill.

Rich City merchants were also coming to Hampstead to build their country houses. We do not know

18. *Fenton House* by Thomas Way, 1898.

which of them to thank for Fenton House, built in 1693, but one of its earliest occupants was a successful silk trader, Joshua Gee, who installed the elaborate wrought-iron gates on Holly Bush Hill. Philip Fenton, who arrived in 1793 and left his name on the house, was a Riga merchant. He and his family took a great interest in Hampstead, and in 1829 rallied protesters against the Lord of the Manor, when he proposed to build on the Heath. Lady Binning bequeathed the house, contents and gardens to the National Trust in 1952, and it is now open to the public. It houses fine pictures, porcelain and furniture, and the Benton Fletcher collection of playable musical instruments, which includes a harpsichord of 1612, once used by Handel. Fenton House remains the oldest surviving mansion in Hampstead.

The modest front block of Burgh House was built in 1703 by a Quaker family called Sewell, another example of non-conformist activity in the area. The property was soon taken over and enlarged by Dr William Gibbons, physician to the Spa which was burgeoning on the doorstep: he added the hind quarters, the handsome staircase and the wrought-iron gates, which include his initials. The Reverend Allatson Burgh, who lived here from 1822–56, was an unpopular Vicar of St Lawrence Jewry. He also treated the house badly, as did his successors, the Royal East Middlesex Militia, who used it as an officers' mess and surrounded it with barrack blocks. Later, kinder occupants included Dr George Williamson, an international art expert (and adviser to Pierpont Morgan), who commissioned Gertrude Jekyll to design the garden (only her terrace remains), and Captain George Bambridge, a retired diplomat, whose wife Elsie was daughter of Rudyard Kipling. The house now belongs to Camden Council, who have leased it to a local charitable trust for community use. Attractions include concerts, lectures, library, art shows, bookstall, Buttery and the Hampstead Museum.

19. Burgh House, drawn by E. Stamp, 1938.

20. The staircase at Burgh House, drawn by E. Stamp, 1938.

A Spa is Born

WELL WALK

Hampstead reached its first heyday in the early 18th century, when its picturesque situation, healthy air and medicinal water combined to turn it into a popular spa. As early as 1697 that tireless traveller, Celia Fiennes, had reported favourably on Hampstead waters, with their 'fine stone bason [*sic*], in which you see the springs bubble up, and by a pipe run off as clear and fast'.

But the following year there was a dramatic development. The Honourable Susannah Noel, acting on behalf of her 13-year-old son, the Earl of Gainsborough, the Lord of the Manor of Hampstead, granted six acres of swampy waste land on the edge of the Heath 'for the sole use, benefit and advantage of the poor of the Parish of Hampstead'. This land, in what is now the Well Walk area, was described as 'lying and being about certain medicinal waters called the Wells', and a Trust was set up to administer the enterprise.

The well water contained iron, and like other chalybeate springs, for instance at Tunbridge Wells, was valued in the treatment of all manner of diseases. Gout and gravel were alleviated, shingles and scrofula banished, bladders and kidneys improved – or so said the Spa doctors at the time. The cynical sneered that the Spa-lovers' cures were as imaginary as their maladies. From 1700 the Trustees had the water bottled at the Flask Tavern, hence the name of the present pub and of Flask Walk, and sold by, among others, an apothecary in Fleet Street at three pence per bottle. The water had an unpleasant metallic flavour that appealed to its drinkers on the grounds that a nastier taste meant a better medicine. Later that year, the Wells Trust found an entrepreneur, John Duffield, to develop the spring's potential as a more lucrative business, and so the Spa began.

Duffield built a ninety-foot Long Room in Well Walk, divided into a small Pump Room with fountain and a large Assembly Room with entertainments. Here visitors could recover from drinking the water and enjoy the recreations provided – concerts, cards, dancing, gambling and refined social dalliance. Nearby were raffling shops, a tavern and the pleasure grounds (now Gainsborough Gardens), where there were shady walks and arbours, a lake and a bowling green.

The Long Room seated five hundred, and Duffield was soon promoting 'particular Consorts of good Musick', at which 'the best Masters of the day' performed. All the latest popular pieces were included, duets by Purcell and songs from the current shows,

21. The first Long Room in Well Walk, from a watercolour by J.P. Emslie, 1879.

22. Baptist Noel, Earl of Gainsborough, Lord of the Manor of Hampstead and benefactor of the local poor; he died of smallpox in 1707, aged 29. From a stipple portrait by Harding, in Barratt's *Annals*.

23. *The Long Room* as a Chapel-of-Ease, c1845; a back view by George Potter.

such as *Chloe Blushed*. Fashionable crowds were attracted to Hampstead not only to take the waters but to enjoy the sophisticated pleasures of the Spa, and perhaps to stay the night. Lodging houses sprang up, especially in the New End area, a brewery was built, and new residential terraces were erected in Church Row and Elm Row.

Among the notable supporters of the Spa was the writer, John Gay, who had a cottage in Hampstead and who found inspiration from the Heath's busy highwaymen for his masterpiece, *The Beggar's Opera*. Poems and ballads were written about the beauties of Hampstead, and in 1707 Thomas Baker's comedy *Hampstead Heath*, was produced successfully at Drury Lane.

But perhaps the greatest stamp of approval came from the Kit-Cat Club. This group of cultured and distinguished Whigs, named after their favourite tavern keeper, Christopher Cat, chose to have its summer meetings at the Upper Flask Tavern, which stood at the top of Heath Street. Here came, among others, Addison and Steele, Vanbrugh and Marlborough, and Sir Godfrey Kneller, whose portraits of them all now hang in the National Portrait Gallery.

Sadly, the Spa became too successful and attracted too many of the wrong people. Its 'nearness to London brings so many loose women in vamped-up old clothes that modest company are ashamed to appear here' warned John Macky in *A Journey through England* of 1714. Daniel Defoe, after a similar tour, reported that 'Hampstead itself has suffered in its good name. Ladies who value their reputation have of late avoided the Wells.'

By 1719 Duffield was seriously in debt, and soon afterwards the Spa closed down. The Long Room was quickly taken over as a chapel-of-ease for the parish church, and a bellcote was added to the roof. The local population was delighted to avoid the long muddy walk to Church Row, where the church was already overcrowded. By 1852, this congregation had built Christ Church for itself and handed over the Spa building to another local group, the Presbyterians. After *they* had erected their chapel in Willoughby Road in 1862, the Long Room was used as a drill hall for the Hampstead Volunteers. It was finally demolished in 1882. The site is now marked by the entrance to Gainsborough Gardens from Well Walk, opposite the Victorian fountain which commemorates the famous chalybeate well.

24. *The Bell at Kilburn*, with tollgate on right, engraved by J. Cary, 1789.

KILBURN AND BELSIZE

Soon after the Spa had expired in Well Walk, other local establishments began organising attractions for the pleasure-loving public.

The Bell Tavern at Kilburn discovered a mineral spring in its back garden in 1714, and soon was advertising 'Kilburn Wells': 'the Waters are now in the utmost perfection, the Gardens beautified in the most elegant manner, the Great Room adapted for the amusement of the politest companies'. They added encouragingly: 'It is most delightfully situated on the site of the once famous Abbey of Kilburn in the Edgware Road at an easy distance, being but a morning's walk from the metropolis. Breakfasting and Hot Loaves.'

Kilburn's popularity was brief, but the pleasure gardens of Belsize Park, without any suggestion of medicinal waters or of doing good to anyone, attracted the crowds for over thirty years. In 1683, Belsize was inherited from Lord Wotton by his half-brother, Philip, the second Earl of Chesterfield. He sub-let the property without any restrictions on a series of life-leases, the first being to Charles Povey, 'a man of scheming and speculative turn'. Povey opened the house for wining, dining, gaming and dancing, and the park for outdoor pursuits such as deer-hunting: there was also a sixpenny lottery for a share of the venison. In the grounds Sion Chapel was available for private weddings at five shillings a time, as long as the wedding feast was held in the gardens.

In 1720 Povey sub-let to an even more enterprising character called Howell, self-styled 'His Excellency the Welsh Ambassador'. To the already long list of attractions, he added duck-hunting, horse-racing, and footman-racing. (You could enter your valet for the 3.30 and bet on him.) Belsize was open most days from 6am to 8pm and the management offered a valuable protection service, which we might still welcome today: 'there will be twelve stout fellows, completely armed, to patrol between London and Belsize'.

Howell's pleasure park reached the height of its fame in 1721, when the Prince and Princess of Wales dined at the house, and in the following year when 'the appearance of nobility and gentry at Belsize was so great that they reckoned between three and four hundred coaches' – presumably in a day. Inevitably, musicians dashed off *The Belsize Minuet* and *The Belsize Ballad*, which began:

Ye beaux who love sporting, young virgins courting,

    Be all resorting to the House of Belsize.

There's kissing and canting, roaring and ranting,

      Sighing and panting, with languishing eyes.

Satirical poems proclaimed that 'Sodom of old was a more righteous place', and Belsize was found to be 'over-boisterous'. Howell was in trouble over gambling and other excesses at Belsize and, after strong protests from local residents, the place was closed down by the magistrates.

To conclude its story, the Belsize estate of 234 acres was sold by the Chesterfield family in 1807, and was bought by a syndicate of four local men. The last notable tenant of the big house was the Prime Minister, Spencer Perceval, whose life is less remembered than his death in 1812, at the hand of an assassin in the House of Commons. The rebuilt version of the house was demolished in 1853 and Belsize Park became, as the *Illustrated London News* said, 'a pleasant, airy suburb'.

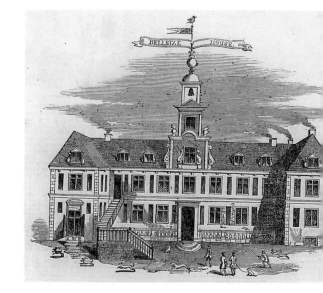

25. *Old Belsize House* from an engraving of *c*1721.

26. *Belsize House*, 1845, engraved for *Pictorial Times*.

27. *A Prospect of the Long Room at Hampstead* by Chatelain, 1745.

28. Chatelain's view of the second Spa, adapted by Wedgwood for Catherine the Great's dinner service, 1774.

WELL WALK AGAIN

As the delights of Belsize dimmed, the fortunes of Hampstead Wells were revived. The rapidly growing town needed recreational facilities, and in the 1730s a second Long Room was built in Well Walk (the old one was still a chapel-of-ease), together with a Ball Room. The only artist to record life at the Spa was a Londoner of French extraction, John Baptist Chatelain, who specialised in landscape engravings, and one of his prints of 1752 (27) shows the new Wells buildings. The view is up what we now call Willow Road, with the Heath beginning of the right. The two long, low, white buildings are the new Long Room on the left, and the Ball Room on the right. Behind the Long Room is Burgh House, home of the Spa doctor. A replica of this panorama was included by Wedgwood in the 950-piece dinner service commissioned from him by Catherine, Empress of Russia, in 1774. This famous 'Green Frog' service, which may still be seen at the Hermitage in Leningrad, had a different view of picturesque Britain on every piece, and as many as a dozen of those views were of Hampstead.

The second Spa was welcomed by a further ballad, but much of its early success was due to the prom-

otional efforts of Dr John Soame. In his *Hampstead Wells or Direction for the Drinking of those Waters* published in 1734, Soame enthused about the Hampstead spring: 'After it has been well cork'd and seal'd down, kept in a Cellar for one or two Years, [the water] sparkled and knit up like a Glass of Champaign or Herefordshire Cyder.' But he also recommended bathing in it, shaving with it and, of course, taking it as medicine.' About the year 1727,' he recalled, 'I was grievously afflicted with the Gravel and Stone, both in my bladder and kidneys…I began to drink the Hampstead Waters regularly, by which means I found myself much relieved. I voided a large

Quantity of Gravel and Sand of a reddish colour, and in a Week's time I voided several small stones, some as big as Peas.'

The Pump Room of the Wells was now in a small building below the Wells Tavern, but residents and visitors showed less interest in the waters, and more and more devotion to the Long Room and Ball Room. Alexander Pope was an early patron of the second Spa, followed later by Oliver Goldsmith and Dr Samuel Johnson. It was his wife's neuroses that brought Johnson to Hampstead, but he sought a cure for them here in vain. He installed her at Priory Lodge in Frognal, and stayed there himself on sever-

29. A musical tribute to fashionable Hampstead, published *c*1737.

Reproduction of " The Beautys of Hampstead " from Bickham's *Musical Entertainer*, about 1737.

al occasions between 1748 and 1752. During one of his visits he wrote most of *The Vanity of Human Wishes*. Priory Lodge was pulled down in the 1920s, when the Frognal Way area was developed.

Another literary light to illuminate the Spa scene was Fanny Burney, who came to Hampstead frequently, and reflected her impressions in her epistolary novel, *Evelina*, published in 1778. On one occasion, the eponymous heroine attended a ball at the Long Room, noting 'this room seems very well named, for I believe it would be difficult to find another epithet which might with propriety distinguish it, as it is without ornament, elegance, or any sort of singularity, and merely to be marked by its length'. The ball was not appreciated either, because Evelina was abandoned by her escort and chaperone, and was accosted by young men 'of

30. *Fanny Burney*, Madame D'Arblay.

31. *Priory Lodge* in Frognal by J.P. Emslie, 1899.

32. The second Spa buildings photographed by Topical Press in 1944, shortly before their demolition.

whom the appearance and language was inelegant and low bred'.

Fashion was deserting Hampstead and in the last quarter of the 18th century the Spa buildings were used less for pleasure and more for community convenience – as a courthouse, for committee rooms, and for meetings of the Loyal Hampstead Association. Soon after 1800 the buildings became private residences, and by then the heady days of Hampstead Wells were a distant memory. A photograph of 1944 *(32)* shows the old Ball Room in its final form, clad in red brick, shuttered and dormered and looking the worse for wear. The caption claims that the building had associations with not only Dr Johnson and Fanny Burney, but with Brahms, who is said to have given recitals of his music there. The air raid shelter on the left of the picture was probably much used, as the old Ball Room and Long room were badly shaken by bombs. They were considered unsalvageable and after the war were demolished. The council flats called Wells House rose in their stead and, in fact, the two blocks facing Well Walk follow the actual site lines of these Spa buildings. There is another souvenir nearby. Some of the 18th-century pine panelling from the Long Room was removed in the late 1920s to line the newly-built Music Room at Burgh House, where 'Consorts of good Music' can still be enjoyed.

High Roads and Low Roads

33. *Pond Street*, the name of the South End Green area in the 1820s, when this engraving was published.

34 *(on following pages)*. Section of *John Rocque's map of London*, 1746.

THE 1746 SCENE

The growth of Hampstead from Stuart village to elegant Georgian town is well shown on the first detailed map of the area by John Rocque in 1746 *(34)*. Compared with the 146 dwellings recorded in a survey exactly a century before, the buildings had more than doubled in number and the resident population increased from about 600 to over 1400. In addition, there was a large floating population of lodgers, weekenders and visitors to the Wells.

The old main thoroughfares of the parish stand out clearly. The long, straight Roman Watling Street in the west, passing through the fields of Kilburn and Shoot-up Hill, was the oldest street in the area. The rambling road through Haverstock Hill, Hampstead town and 'Groles Green' was the alternative high-level route. Three important lanes linked up the communities.

West End Lane ran from Kilburn Abbey on Watling Street, through West End village, to meet Childs Hill and North End. Shoot-up Hill Lane (now Mill Lane) led from the windmill on the main road (marked above the words Shoot Up) via West End Lane (now partly Frognal Lane) to the Manor Farm at Frognal. Belsize Lane wandered from West End, via Belsize House and its pentagonal park, to Pond (misspelt Pound) Street, which was an old-established settlement. Notably missing from the map are Finchley Road and Fitzjohns Avenue, which did not appear until the next century. Hampstead High Street appears to head for North End via Holly Hill, Hampstead Grove and the West Heath behind Jack Straw's Castle, while Heath Street leads only to 'Spaniards Gate' and the north east, but it is known that the North End Way cutting was already in use by then. The Wells buildings, Burgh House, Admiral's House, Judges Walk and other present features of Hampstead can be identified on this helpful but not entirely accurate map. Its main pleasure and surprise is to see Hampstead surrounded by heath, pasture and arable, and the now 'lost' rivers flowing by.

35. A view of Hampstead from the footway next the Great Road Pond Street, engraved by Chatelain in 1752.

HIGH ROAD

Turnpike trusts were introduced in England from the late 17th century to build and repair specific stretches of road, financed by tolls collected from the users. One of the earliest toll gates in Hampstead was set up on the Edgware Road, roughly where Kilburn High Road now takes over from Maida Vale. The Kilburn toll bar was still there in the early 1880s, just before turnpikes were phased out and local councils made responsible for road maintenance. Toll charges were normally a farthing per head of cattle, a penny per wheel of a vehicle, and sixpence for a carriage horse. Church traffic for weddings or funerals was exempt.

Kilburn High Road stretches from the Westminster border to Brondesbury, and contains the ancient foundations of several taverns, now totally rebuilt. The Red Lion was established in 1444, but the present pub dates from 1890. The Olde Bell, whose tea gardens were a feature of Kilburn Wells, originated about 1600 and was rebuilt in 1863. Towards Brondesbury the Black Lion claims a starting date of 1666: it was rebuilt in a flamboyant Flemish Gothic style in 1898, and is now the only Listed Building in the road. Most of the grander old houses on the street have disappeared, including Clarence House, where Thomas Hardy lodged in the 1860s: he was then an architectural assistant to (Sir) Arthur Blomfield.

UP HAVERSTOCK HILL

The name of Haverstock Hill was originally applied only to the settlement that grew up around its first steep slope, as shown on Rocque's map of 1746. The tremendous view across London, with St Paul's in the distance, was captured by Constable in a painting of 1832, called *Steele's Cottage (37)*. This picturesque cottage is on the right, named after the essayist, Sir Richard Steele, who took refuge here in 1712. For him it was conveniently far from his creditors in the City, and pleasantly near to upper Hampstead where the Kit-Cat Club met. The house was demolished in 1867, but the writer is well commemorated in Steele's Road, Mews and Studios, and the Sir Richard Steele public house.

Across the road, and only just visible in the picture in its pre-Victorian version, is the Load of Hay. Washington Irving described the Irish haymakers and the drovers who used this pub in his *Tales of a Traveller*. For many years this tavern was a regular stopping place for coaches and carters, whose horses found the steepness of the hill such a strain. It was rebuilt in 1863 and is now a Listed Building. In 1965 it was temporarily re-christened The Noble Art, because of its popular boxing gymnasium.

Haverstock is a curious name that has not been definitively explained. It probably comes from the

36. *Kilburn High Road* in the Brondesbury area, a late Victorian postcard.

37. *Sir Richard Steele's Cottage*, Haverstock Hill, engraved by David Lucas from a painting of 1832 by John Constable.

38. The Toll Bar at Kilburn in 1881, from a painting by Frank Sparks.

Anglo-Saxon, meaning the place of oats – and we know that payment in oats was part of Belsize manor's rent to Westminster Abbey in Tudor times.

Haverstock Hill turns into Rosslyn Hill at the junction with Pond Street, and Chatelain recorded the view uphill from here in 1752. *(38)* The main road with its coach and horses, and a drove of cattle, is separated by a hedge from the pedestrian precinct on the right. There are even bollards halfway up the hill to discourage wheeled traffic. This stretch of road, originally known as Red Lion Hill after an ancient pub on its western side, was renamed in the early 19th century to commemorate the local residence of Lord Chancellor Wedderburn, Earl of Rosslyn.

The oldest known well in Hampstead village was called the King's Well. Robert de Kyngeswell was recorded as a free tenant of Hampstead manor in 1312, and Kingswell Street was the first name for what is now Hampstead High Street. This road has gradually narrowed over the years, as shops and pavements were extended, except in its top section, which was widened in 1888.

Many of the modern shop fronts on both sides of the High Street conceal ancient buildings, some of

39 and 40. Two postcard views of the High Street in the 1930s, from watercolours by Mary Hill.

which still have Tudor beams. The new Post Office is on the site of one of the oldest rows of houses on the west side. From 1883 to 1938 they were used as the offices of the prestigious *Hampstead and Highgate Express* and, after that, as motor showrooms. Next door, the admirable Hampstead Community Centre has taken over the old stables, later garage, of the adjoining William IV. This inn, probably of 17th-century origin, changed its name from the King's Head after King William passed through Hampstead in 1835. His queen, Adelaide, was commemorated by a tavern and a road at the foot of the hill.

Heath Street climbs narrowly to the brow of Hampstead Hill and there you can look back and see it much as George Shepherd saw it in 1830 *(42)*. There is the wide raised pavement and railings, and there in the middle are the tall Regency buildings, one of which has half a millstone (one of Hampstead's?) built into its steps. The wall on the right still has a similar kink, but the house behind has disappeared.

This was Heath Mount School, which was founded in 1790 'for the sons of gentlemen', and flourished here until 1934, when the school moved out to Hertfordshire. Among its pupils were some distinguished local boys, such as (Sir) Gerald du Maurier, (Sir) Cecil Beaton and Evelyn Waugh.

At the crest of the hill, on a sunny weekend, you will find Whitestone Pond as a hub of tourist activity, of traffic tangles and of such happy paddling and model-boating that have earned it the nickname of Hampstead-on-Sea. Until recently Windsor Castle was still visible on the skyline, but trees and tower blocks have intervened. The south-eastern outlook over the Vale of Health to Blackheath and beyond remains splendid. The pond's history is of a small dew pond, supplemented by rainwater, which grew in Victorian times to a valuable horse pond. Ramps at either end allowed horse-drawn vehicles to be driven through the water, which provided a much-needed coolant for horses after their long pull up hill. Their

41. The recently demolished Adelaide Tavern at the junction of Haverstock Hill and Adelaide Road, an Edwardian photograph.

42. *Heath Mount* by George Shepherd, 1830.

43. *Whitestone Pond*, a turn-of-the century photograph.

44. *North End*, lithograph by T.M. Baynes, 1822.

drivers were refreshed at the adjoining tavern.

The pond's name derives from the white milestone, once near the middle of the road but now in a clump of bushes to the south. Its inscriptions read: '4½ miles from Holborn Bars' and 'IV miles from St Giles's Pound'. (This pound was near the site of today's Centre Point building.) Our turn-of-the-century photograph *(43)* shows Christ Church spire on the right and, near the centre, Bellmoor, the home of Thomas J. Barratt, author of *The Annals of Hampstead*.

North End Way descends through a cutting, probably dating from the 1730s, to Hampstead's northern border. Here is the hamlet of North End which is presumed to have been the Sandgate mentioned in Ethelred's charter of AD986: the Sandy Heath begins here. Camden's *Britannia* and other documents of the 16th and 17th centuries refer to the settlement as

NOV 0 THE HOUSE IN WHICH GREAT BRITAIN LOST AMERICA: NORTH-END PLACE, HAMPSTEAD HEATH.

It was to North-End Place that William Pitt, first Earl of Chatham, withdrew to shut himself off from public life. Had the great statesman, instead of being in retirement there, been in health and in his place, the Boston tea-tax would almost certainly not have been imposed, and the Union Jack would probably have been flying over America to-day. So determined was Pitt to be alone that his meals were served to him through a hole in the wall, shown in our Illustration. Of this Mr. F. E. Baines wrote: "In the door of this room, in the upper right hand panel, was placed the food-box. From the outside the meals were put into the box by a servant, the occupant of the room being hidden from view; and when the footsteps of the servant had died away, the invalid withdrew the dishes from within." The property is to be sold by auction, at the Mart, on Tuesday next (the 17th) by Messrs. Lowe, Goldschmidt and Howland, of Heath Street, Hampstead.—[DRAWN BY W. B. ROBINSON.]

45. *North End Place* or Pitt House, from a magazine of 1908.

Wildwood Corner which, along with the name Wyldes for the local farm, suggests a clearing in a largely untamed woodland. The herbalist, John Gerard, reported finding white butterfly orchids here in 1597. Behind the two famous pubs, the Bull and Bush and the Hare and Hounds, are a number of elegant houses, including Byron Cottage, named after the wealthy Lady Byron who came to live here in 1908. She was the wife of the ninth Lord Byron, familiarly known as 'red-nosed George', and only distantly related to the poet. Lady Byron, who remarried and became Lady Houston, contributed such large sums in the 1930s towards the development of the Spitfire aircraft that she was dubbed by her biographer 'the Woman who won the War'. Other distinguished residents of North End have been the ballerina, Anna Pavlova, who lived on the Hendon side of the border, and Sir Nikolaus Pevsner, the architectural historian and creator of forty-seven volumes of *The Buildings of England*.

Nothing now remains of the most important house in this area, once known as North End Place, but latterly as Pitt House. Here in 1767 came a mentally sick Prime Minister, William Pitt, Earl of Chatham, hoping in vain that solitude would cure his ills. Meals were served through a hatch and a box cupboard, which Pitt would open only when the servant had retired. Had the Prime Minister recovered his health, some said, he would have resisted the imposition of the American tea tax, the Boston Tea Party would not have taken place and, perhaps, the American Colonies would have remained part of the British Empire.

For Richer, For Poorer

CHURCH ROW

One of the earliest effects of the successful Spa on village Hampstead was the creation of more sophisticated accommodation both for residents and visitors. Statelier homes with large grounds were erected and terraces sprang up in New End, Elm Row and, most happily, Church Row.

46. Church Row. Nos. 22–28, photographed in 1932.

Turning your back on the Victorian mansion flats and ignoring the traffic, you can enjoy the sweep of early 18th-century houses on both sides of the Row, with the parish church towering at the far end. It is the handsomest street in Hampstead. Although many of the houses have been altered or refaced or have lost their railings, there is still a wealth of Georgian detail in the fanlights, canopies and wrought-iron work. The lack of uniformity in height, width and design of the houses is part of the street's curiosity and attraction. No. 5 is white and weatherboarded. No. 8, once home of the writer, Mrs Barbauld, is tall and narrow, while no. 9 was large enough to house a Girls' Reformatory School in the 1860s.

H.G. Wells and his family lived at no. 17 before the 1st World War while, at much the same time, Lord Alfred Douglas and his wife were residing at no. 26. George du Maurier had his first Hampstead house at no. 27, with a Home for the Rescue of Young Women next door. No. 28 was later the offices of the busy local builder, C.B. King, who repaired and refaced much of the street, and who left his mark in the brickwork of no. 24, a fleur-de-lys.

Until the end of the 19th century the northern part of Church Row was private property and access to Frognal was controlled by a tollgate. The land belonged to the Old Mansion in Frognal, whose grounds stretched from Church Row to Mount Vernon: they were big enough to encompass the whole of Frognal Gardens, laid out in 1889. The tollgate was the last to disappear from Hampstead's streets.

47. Tollgate in Church Row, c1899.

48. View of Hampstead Church from Frognal with Frognal Hall
on the right and London in the distance; aquatint after
Thomas Stowers, 1796.

49. The Parish Church by C.J. Greenwood, *c*1857.

On the site of the medieval church of St Mary, the new parish church of St John-at-Hampstead was consecrated in October 1747. Nobody recorded which St John was intended, so the church's west window shows both the Evangelist and the Baptist, and the two patronal days are celebrated. The architect was John Sanderson, who lived near the Spaniards Inn. In the 1840s transepts were added and the interior was lavishly decorated. A print of *c*1857 shows the altar at the east end, below the elaborate commandment boards, together with a grandiose pulpit and lectern. In 1878 further enlargements were made to provide accommodation for about 1400 people. In the same year the whole church was reorientated, so that the main entrance was transferred conveniently to the east end, and the altar to the west. As the church guide comments: 'It thus resembles St Peter's in Rome and a number of continental churches, but is highly unusual in England.'

Among the interesting monuments in the church is a bust of Keats, presented by American admirers of the poet in 1894; it is said by Barratt to be 'the first memorial to Keats raised on English soil'. The most important tomb in the picturesque graveyard is that of the artist, John Constable, and his family, who lived at no. 40 Well Walk and other Hampstead addresses for many years. Another fine Georgian chest tomb belongs to John Harrison, 'Inventor of the Time Keeper for ascertaining the Longitude at Sea'. In the churchyard extension are the graves of, among other eminent local residents, George and Gerald du Maurier, Hugh Gaitskell, Cyril Joad, E.V. Knox and Beerbohm Tree. The graveyard's 2,500 or so inscriptions have recently been recorded by the Camden History Society and evaluated in their publication *Buried in Hampstead*.

THE RICH

Rosslyn House, near the top of Lyndhurst Road, was demolished in 1896 after a long and fairly distinguished career. Over the years the original Tudor house had been rebuilt and extended with bow fronts and wings, part Georgian, part classical, until it was more a curiosity than a beauty. From the 17th century the property had belonged to the Chesterfield family, who owned the whole Belsize Estate.

50. Rosslyn House being demolished 1896, watercolour by J.P. Emslie.

51. *The Soldiers' Daughters School* drawn by its architect, William Munt. This building, which was behind Vane House, is now Fitzjohns Primary School.

52. *Alexander Wedderburn* (1733–1805), 1st Baron Loughborough and 1st Earl of Rosslyn, a contemporary engraving.

With its large grounds and handsome grove of Span-ish chestnuts, making an avenue from Rosslyn Hill, the house attracted some important tenants, none more so than Alexander Wedderburn in 1793, newly created Lord Chancellor.

Wedderburn was a Scots barrister who quickly rose to become Chief Justice of Common Pleas in 1780, the year of the Gordon Riots. Created the first Baron Loughborough in the same year, Wedderburn dealt so harshly with the rioters that he was called 'the second Judge Jeffreys'. Rosslyn House was then called Grove House, but Wedderburn renamed it Shelford Lodge after a Chesterfield property in Not-tinghamshire. He left Hampstead in 1802 after retir-ing from the Chancellorship and being created Earl of Rosslyn in consolation.

His successor as tenant, Robert Milligan, cham-pion of the West India Docks, probably renamed the Lodge 'Rosslyn House'. Among its later admirers were Queen Victoria, who considered taking it as a nursery for the royal children, and Prince Albert, who came when it was used as the Royal Soldiers' Daughters Home.'A large, commodious house at

53. *Branch Hill Lodge* by Thomas Way, 1899.

Hampstead' had been needed urgently in the 1850s to shelter some of the soldiers' daughters orphaned by the Crimean War. (Sailors' Daughters were housed in Frognal.) Rosslyn House happened to be vacant at the time and seventy girls were accommodated here and trained, largely for domestic service. In 1858 a more suitable mansion was made available at Vane House and Prince Albert led the girls in procession up Rosslyn Hill to their new home.

Before taking Rosslyn House, Alexander Wedderburn had stayed for some years at Branch Hill Lodge at the top of Frognal. This property, known as Bleak Hall in the 18th century, had long associations with lawyers. In 1745 Sir Thomas Clarke, the pawnbroker's son who became Master of the Rolls, had the house redesigned by the great Henry Flitcroft, then resident in Frognal. There followed the family of Sir Thomas Parker, a fraudulent judge, and Thomas Walker, a Master in Chancery.

Later residents included Lady Byron, who rented the house soon after her separation from the poet. In 1867 the Lodge was much altered by S.S. Teulon, architect of St Stephen's, Rosslyn Hill, who also designed the present gatehouse. The estate was finally sold in 1965 to Camden Council, who turned the house into an old people's home and the grounds into a council estate. The development was an imaginative but expensive one. The site was steep and remote and plagued by unstable soil, dumped here from the excavation of the Northern Line. The resulting forty-two dwellings were said at the time to be the costliest council houses ever built.

One of the small terraces that resulted from the Spa's population explosion was much truncated in the last century, leaving only Stanfield House, now at the corner of the High Street and Prince Arthur Road. The handsome original terrace of three houses was built about 1730, probably by the Key family, which had made its fortune from wholesale stationery. The artist, Clarkson Stanfield, RA, took the northernmost house, on which he has left his name, in 1847. Press-ganged into the navy at an early age,

Stanfield had specialised successfully in nautical pictures, but he was also in demand to design stage scenery. Among his close friends and patrons was Charles Dickens, for whose amateur theatricals he created the set of *The Lighthouse*, still preserved at Dickens House in Holborn. In 1865 Stanfield and his large family were driven out by the development of Prince Arthur Road, which resulted in two thirds of the terrace being demolished. The remaining house was thereafter devoted to a life of public service. After a few years as a Consumption Hospital, while Mount Vernon Hospital was being built, Stanfield House was converted to the Hampstead Subscription Library. The hall at the back was added as a reading room by Horace Field. Earlier this century other parts of the building were used by local societies – historical, astronomical and archaeological and, after the last war, included a Christian Science Church.'This rather gaggly house,' as a sales advertisement of the 1970s put it, has now been

54. *Stanfield House* in its original terrace, drawing by George Stanfield, son of Clarkson, *c*1860.

largely redomesticated.

Two grand houses were built to the north of the Wells in the early 18th century and have happily survived, though much altered. Cannon Hall, dating from about 1720, took its name from the old cannon embedded in the pavement outside: once useful as hitching posts for horses, they are now a helpful deterrent to pavement parkers. The Hall's most famous inhabitant was the actor-manager and matinee idol Sir Gerald du Maurier. He lived here from 1916 until his death in 1934; his daughter, Daphne, the novelist, was brought up here. On the other side of Cannon Lane is Squire's Mount, seen in our photograph (*61*) in the occupation of another matinee idol and film star of the 1930s, Clive Brook.

Squire's Mount was built in 1714 by Joshua Squire as a terrace of four houses. This later became two residences, one part now called Chestnut Lodge, with a neo-Georgian addition by Horace Field. After a period as Mrs Holt's School for Young Ladies, the house was taken in the 1850s by Edwin Field, the law reformer and art patron: Turner was among his distinguished circle. After Field died in 1871, rescuing a man drowning in the Thames, his daughters stayed on at Squire's Mount until the 1920s, finally leaving the property to the National Trust.

55. Sir Gerald du Maurier and his daughter, Daphne, who lived at Cannon Hall.

56. The Gibbet Elms near North End by George Barnard, 1844.

THE POOR

The opening of Hampstead's first workhouse in the midsummer of 1729 was probably as much welcomed by the poor of the parish as by the ratepayers. The local paupers, whose numbers had risen rapidly with the fame of the Spa, had hitherto been accommodated in individual 'poorhouses'. These were mostly crumbling cottages, where the poor lived, as a contemporary writer reported, 'in nastiness as well as poverty'. Their rent and weekly allowance of a few shillings were financed by the local Poor Rate, which was a stiff one shilling and sixpence in the pound.

By renting a large, old house in Frognal, which could take twenty or more inmates at a time, the Vestry (parish council) was able to reduce the Poor Rate to 10d, and provide better conditions for the paupers. Unlike the notorious workhouse at St Pancras, the Hampstead institution was considered a remarkably humanitarian establishment. Account books have survived from the 1730s to show that supplies of food were reasonable and included a surprising amount of meat. Fresh vegetables were grown by the inmates in the workhouse grounds, and some of these were sold locally to defray institutional costs. Another job creation scheme for the women and children was the making of mops, evidently not very profitable but, as a supervisor remarked, 'infinitely preferable to idleness and beggary'.

From the 1750s financial considerations prompted periods of closure for the workhouse and the re-introduction of the poorhouse scheme. Three small houses near Jack Straw's Castle were rented for this purpose, but soon after the Vale of Health area was drained in 1777 the paupers were transferred there. As far as is known they were the first inhabitants of this now desirable locality, and an 1804 print shows little in the Vale except the poor houses and the pond *(59)*.

In 1801 a new workhouse was established in New End which, rebuilt and extended over the years, grew into New End Hospital. The decorated central block was built in the 1840s, the water tower and innovative circular wards (now a Listed Building) in 1883–4, and the final main extension up to Heath Street in 1905 *(60)*. The building was used not only as

57. Alms House, Frognal by J.P. Malcolm, 1797.

House Charge From y
19th of Jan. to y 26: 1735.

Eatables   £ = S = d

pd for Milk — — — — 0: 1= 0
pd for Bakeing Beef & puding 0= 0= 2
pd ale for Mr Waters — — — 0: 0: 1
pd for Turnops & Carrots — 0 0: 3½
pd Mr Snoxcol for 27 of Pork 0: 6: 9
pd for Bakeing pork & Potates, 0: 0: 2
                 0= 8=5½
, of Mr Vincent, 1 Bar. of Beer- 0—7-0
, of Mr Emens, 1 Lo & Peck of Flour 0 = 10:10
, of Mrs Lucas Mutt & suett — 1½ 0: 3: 3
, of Mr Dobson, f: 3/ : & 2 Ounces — 0= 2: 6
and 4d of Butter — — — — 0: 2- 0
and Cours Sugar 3d — — 0: 1: 0
and 2d of Rice — — — — 0: 0: 6
and Spice, 2: ounes, & 2 ounces 0: 0: 6
             1—1½=0½

58. Page from a Workhouse accounts book, 1735.

a workhouse, but as offices for the town council until the new Town Hall was built in Haverstock Hill in 1877.

Up to two hundred paupers could eventually be accommodated at New End and the jobs they were given to do, deliberately disagreeable, included corn-grinding, wood-chopping and oakum picking. Traditionally men were put to breaking stones for road-mending before they were allowed breakfast, and the resulting fragments had to be small enough to pass through the iron grille on the workshop window. Idleness, blasphemy and waste of provisions were punished by solitary confinement or 'abatement of diet'.

During the 1st World War, when there were jobs for all, the workhouse was discontinued and the building taken over as a military hospital. It remained a hospital after the war and achieved some fame in the 1940s when Sir Geoffrey Keynes was pioneering thyroid surgery here. More recently the hospital became the geriatric wing of the Royal Free, but the whole institution at New End finally closed in 1985. Discussions about the future of this prime site are currently raging.

59. *A View on Hampstead Heath, looking towards London* by F.J. Sarjent, 1804.

60. *New End Hospital*, an undated postcard.

61. *Clive Brook* among the splendours of Squire's Mount, 1939, photographed for *Homes and Gardens*. (*See page 47*)

HIGHWAYMEN

Legends about the highwaymen who flourished on Hampstead Heath have grown up around the taverns they are said to have frequented and around the sinister 'gibbet elms'. These two tall trees, one of which survived until 1907, stood to the north of Jack Straw's Castle, and from a beam between their boughs was hung in chains the body of the notorious Francis Jackson. A vicious robber and killer, Jackson had been caught at North End, and was tried and hanged on the spot. That was in 1673, but his bones were left to rattle for another eighteen years to remind passers-by that crime does not pay. The lesson was not learned by Claude Duval, who was active at the same time in the Platts Lane area. The lane was once known as Duval's Lane, which became corrupted into Devil's Lane before Mr Platt came along to improve its image. Duval achieved brief fame by halting coaches and dancing with the lady passengers while making the gentlemen hand over their valuables.

Even more romanticised, as in the fiction of Harrison Ainsworth, was Dick Turpin (1705–39), who was doubtless attracted to Hampstead by its rich Spa visitors. His is the name most used on bars of Hampstead hostelries, such as the Bull and Bush and Jack Straw's Castle. But the claims of association have mainly come from the Spaniards Inn. Here Turpin was supposed to have stabled his Black Bess, and to have had a special key to a secret passage prepared for his escape. He was said to have watched for coaches being halted at the tollgate and to have noted which were worth robbing in the very near future. There is now no evidence to support any of this, but the legends live on.

The Burgeoning Town

THE 1814 SCENE

In 1814 John James Park, a precocious 19-year-old, produced the first serious history of our area, *The Topography and Natural History of Hampstead*. We know little about the author, except that he lived with his father, Thomas Park, FSA, 'the poetical anti-quary', at no. 18 Church Row, where a private pla-que salutes them both, and that he died in Brighton in 1833.

Fortunately for us, Park's erudite tome, which went to a second, enlarged edition in 1818, included a detailed map of Hampstead *(63)*, surveyed for him by J. & W. Newton, and this gives us a clear picture of the growing town on the eve of Waterloo. Of special interest is the 'Telegraph' marked top left, which reflects Hampstead's involvement in the Napoleonic Wars. As an early warning system for a possible invasion, Telegraph Hill was used as a signalling station by the army in 1798–9, and again by the Admiralty in 1808–14. The line of communication, using a semaphore of either discs or shutters, led to Woodcock Hill in Harrow, similar to the signal chain set up at the time of the Armada.

The war also brought a stream of refugees from the French Revolution to settle in Hampstead. Two years after this map appeared, St Mary's Church was built in Holly Place, mainly by and for these settlers: it is the second oldest Roman Catholic church in London. Among French refugees who came to worship here in the last war was General de Gaulle, a temporary resident of Frognal.

Among the few houses named on the map is Heath Lodge, near North End, which was built in 1775 by the leading actress, Mrs Lessingham, despite protests that it intruded on the Heath. The house was acquired in 1911 by Lord Leverhulme, who was then living in the neighbouring property, and its landscaped grounds have become the Hill Garden. In the south, only Rosslyn House and Belsize House are named.

The importance of Frognal, which terminates just below Church Row, is emphasised by its capital let-ters on the map. At its junction with West End (now Frognal) Lane were the old manorial buildings, in-cluding barns and yards for the Hall Oak or Manor

62. (Below) St Mary's, Holly Place, from a watercolour by Mary Hill, *c*1911.

63. (Facing) Map of Hampstead in 1814, published with J.J. Park's *Topography of Hampstead*.

St Mary's, Holly Place,
HAMPSTEAD.

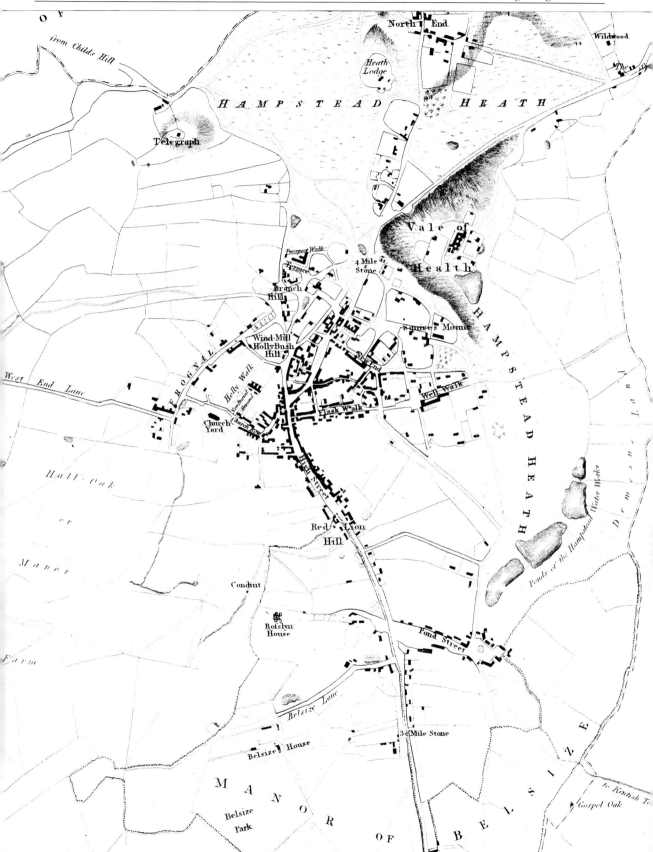

64. *Beating the Bounds,* a souvenir drawing of 1896.

Farm. No Lord of the Manor ever lived in Hampstead, but from early times his headquarters and his bailiff's office was at this crossroads in Frognal.

Note two other features on the map. 'Conduit' is Shepherd's Well, the pure spring that was also the source of the River Tyburn, and 'Gospel Oak' shows where a gospel passage was read during the annual beating of the bounds – a feature which provided a place name.

WEST END

In the middle of the 18th century West End was a hamlet of about forty small houses clustered around West End Green. This was a farming settlement with lanes connecting it with the mills of central Hampstead and Shoot Up Hill, and with Kilburn Priory, which originally ran the farm. In addition, there were two stately homes, West End House, the home of the Beckford family, and West End Hall which, together with the old tavern, the Cock and Hoop, dominated the neighbourhood's life.

The Hall dated back probably to the 17th century and, apart from being the oldest building, became the grandest and most influential. The Miles family, who lived there from 1813 to 1889, took a benevolent squirearchal interest in the community, with particular concern for the welfare and educational needs of the poor. It was they who in 1844 persuaded Hampstead parish church to take pity on West End children, who had a long weary trudge uphill to their classes, and to build a school near the Green.

One of the smallest National Schools in the area, Emmanuel School, as we now know it, consisted of one classroom and a cottage for the mistress. The buildings and playground were squeezed onto one tenth of an acre of land, donated by the tenant of Cholmley Lodge, and enfranchised by the Lord of the Manor: the total cost was £585. It was reckoned that each of the original 143 children had six square

65. *West End* by H. Fancourt, *c*1840, with the Cock and Hoop on the right and West End Hall, centre.

66. *Emmanuel School*, Mill Lane, in the 19th century.

67. *Lauriston Lodge*, a 19th-century watercolour.

68. *The Grange*, off Kilburn High Road.

feet of space. Further ground has since been acquired in Mill Lane and much has been rebuilt, but the premises have kept the intimate aspect of a village school.

West End had been so peaceful at the beginning of the 19th century that the Miles family could set their clocks from the striking of Big Ben, and in 1815 they claimed further that they could hear the cannon at Waterloo. This rural retreat was soon invaded by city merchants and others after country houses, and a number of spacious mansions, such as Treherne House, grew up along West End Lane. The oldest of these, Lauriston Lodge, was the home of the magistrate Germain Lavie, who was instrumental in suppressing the West End Fair. An annual three-day event in July, the Fair began as, in Lavie's words, 'four or five Toy and gingerbread Booths only and a single Show', but a local cowkeeper allowed it to overflow into a nearby field. From 1812 there was increasing opposition to the event, which was now attracting 'London roughs' in large gangs. But it was not until 1821 that the magistrates were able to close it down. Witnesses had described appalling scenes of theft and violence, of clothes cut from people's backs and a gang's brutal assault on a man who escaped only because they threw him through a musicians' tent and the fiddlers joined him in fighting off the attackers.

Further west, on Kilburn High Road, The Grange was a rambling building with a mixture of styles. It was demolished in 1910 but its grounds of eight acres have survived as Grange Park. At its final auction the property was variously claimed to have been the residence of Catherine of Aragon, the shooting box of Charles II and another of Dick Turpin's hideouts. None of these pretensions has been verifiable. Sir Oswald Stoll had plans for developing the estate with a Kilburn Coliseum, on the lines of his theatre in St Martin's Lane. His project was thwarted by Hampstead Council backed, among others, by local schools, who petitioned that 'the attendance of young people at places of entertainment three or four times a week could not fit them for the work they would have to do in life'.

SOUTH END

A large estate between Hampstead Town Centre and the settlement around South End Green had the good fortune to be developed in Regency times. The triangle of handsome houses, embracing Downshire Hill, Keats Grove and South End Road, originated about 1814, and parts appeared on the map of that date published with Park's history.

Downshire Hill displays a wide variety of Regency styles, bow fronts and balconies, Gothic and crenellated or Georgian sober-sided; all the early villas are attractive and have miraculously survived. A splendid centrepiece to this development, St John's Church, was consecrated in 1823. It was probably intended as a chapel-of-ease to the parish church, as

69. Downshire Hill, 1842, by J. & F. Harwood. Note St Michael's, Highgate, on the skyline.

was the Well Walk chapel but, possibly because of a dispute between the incumbents of Downshire Hill and Church Row, it became a proprietary chapel. It is now the last privately-owned church in London. The builder-architect was William Woods of Kennington, who built many of the surrounding houses, using bricks made on the site.

Dante Gabriel Rossetti spent part of his honeymoon in Downshire Hill, and other artists active here included Constable at no. 25, Sir Roland Penrose at no. 36, and the Carline family at no. 47. A frequent visitor was Stanley Spencer, who married Hilda Carline. Other remarkable residents included the poet Edwin Muir at no. 7, writers Robert and Sylvia Lynd at no. 14, the actress Flora Robson at no. 37, and the architect Sir Frederick Gibberd at no. 49. The glass house at no. 49a, designed by Michael Hopkins, won a Civic Trust Award in 1979.

Keats Grove was originally called Albion Grove and, for many years, John Street: it was not until 1910 that the road was named after its most famous resident. John Keats, who had been introduced to Hampstead by Leigh Hunt, came here in 1818 after his brother Tom had died at their lodgings in Well Walk. Keats House, as we know it, was then a newly-built duplex villa with two separate dwellings. The poet shared one of these with his friend Charles Armitage Brown, and from 1819 his beloved Fanny Brawne and her family occupied the other.

70. *John Keats* from a miniature by Joseph Severn, 1818.

71. *Keats House*, an undated, misspelt postcard.

This was the year of his most sublime poetry, including *Ode to a Nightingale*, which he wrote sitting under a plum tree in his garden. Consumed with tuberculosis, he was fo·ced to leave Hampstead and to seek a cure in Italy – he died in Rome in 1821. A hundred years later his house here was threatened by demolition and rescued only by public subscription, mostly from America.

The upper stretch of South End Road has a terrace of Regency cottages, built for the workers and mainly occupied by them until the 1920s. The lower part is dominated by the terrace of shops erected in 1898. On the other side the Heath sweeps down to its southern limit and ends in a grove of trees, which marks the site of the lowest pond. By the 1890s this pond had become a public nuisance, especially to commuters using Hampstead Heath Station, and it was filled in.

The Hampstead and Highgate ponds were reservoirs of water from the River Fleet, used to increase London's often inadequate water supply and, since 1692, they were controlled by the Hampstead Water Company. To boost this supply the Company sank a well in South End Road in 1835, and later deepened it to 470ft. The steam pumping engine was housed in an octagonal tower, seen in our photograph *(72)*, and this functioned until about 1870, when the New River Company took over. The pepperpot building then became a private house until subsidence prompted its demolition in 1907.

72. South End Road, c1905, looking north from Hampstead Heath Station.

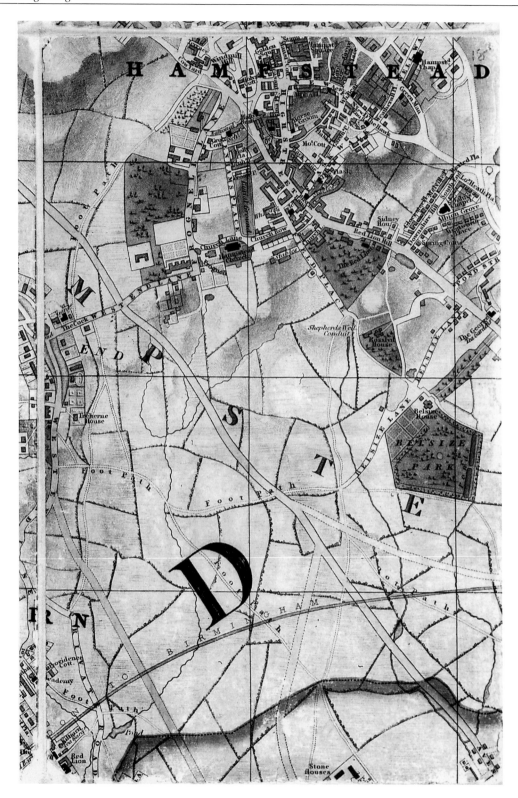

73. *(Facing)* Part of Cruchley's folding map of 1829.

74. *The Swiss Cottage* in 1845, from Barratt's *Annals*.

FINCHLEY ROAD

When Colonel Henry Samuel Eyre was developing his St John's Wood estate about 1820, his grandest plan was for a turnpike trust to build a major highway to Finchley. Angry opposition was immediately voiced by the Lord of the Manor of Hampstead, who feared that his property might be devalued, and by a number of his influential tenants. Local residents were alarmed at the thought that their privacy would be 'disturbed and diminished if by a new Road, as designed, the idle or pleasurable (not to say vicious) members of the Metropolis are to be drawn to Hampstead for objects of pleasure or crime'. All objections were crushed by an Act of Parliament of 1826 which allowed the building of Finchley Road.

Cruchley's *New Plan of London* in 1829 shows that progress was slow. A ghostly thoroughfare winds its way from Regent's Park across the meadows to the north, carefully by-passing West End and Hampstead town. Note the footpath coming south from Shepherd's Well to the new road – this shows the line of the future Fitzjohns Avenue.

A toll-gate was set up at what we now call Swiss Cottage but the first tavern of that name was not built until about 1840. The Swiss style was then much in fashion, owing to the popularity of a new opera called *Le Chalet*, by Adolphe Adam. By 1856 this busy

75. *Swiss Cottage*, looking south down Wellington Road in the 1890s.

76. *Swiss Cottage*, looking north and east in the 1890s.

crossroads had become a terminus for horse buses and in 1868 it acquired an Underground station, on the Metropolitan and St John's Wood Railway, and later a fire station. Having paid for itself handsomely, Finchley Road's toll-gate was removed in 1873 and the road, generously planted with sycamore, elm and plane trees in 1889, was hailed by one admirer as 'the most imposing avenue near London'.

Two panoramic photographs from the 1890s show traffic at Swiss Cottage. In the view southwards (75)

can be seen (left to right) the Dairy, established in 1849, the Tavern, advertising tea gardens behind, and a queue of horse buses stretching down Wellington Road. The extensive mews and stables needed to accommodate the buses, horses and some of the crews were off Fairfax Road.

Looking north the other photograph (76) shows on the left a horse cab-rank in Finchley Road, with New College behind. The castellated College, which inspired the street-name College Crescent, was a non-

conformist theological establishment built at great expense in 1850, but demolished in 1934. A newer New College was then erected higher up Finchley Road, which has now also closed and been taken over by the Open University. The shops in the centre of the photograph have also gone, as has the towering bank building. On the right of Eton Avenue, at no. 100 Avenue Road, is the ornate School for the Blind, which was demolished after the last war. Only the tavern has survived for 150 years and kept its original disguise as a homely Swiss Cottage, albeit frequently rebuilt.

77. *The Swiss Cottage* tavern kitchen in 1912.

78. Primrose Hill Tunnel, drawn by J.F. Burrell, *c*1850.

THE FIRST RAILWAY

In 1837, a few years before the building of Adelaide
Road, the London and Birmingham Railway dug its
way through the southern slopes of Hampstead, despite storms of protest from local organisations. The
Primrose Hill or Chalk Farm Tunnel *(78)* was a major
engineering achievement and the turreted stone por-
tals at either end, designed by Robert Stephenson's
secretary, W.H. Budden, were widely praised. They
also reassured the railway's passengers on the solid-
ity of the tunnel's construction. Elaborate signalling
systems, involving bells to be rung and flags to be
waved by the tunnel keeper, gave further confi-
dence. After the 1830s the London North Western
Railway increased the number of tracks and tunnels
and rebuilt the entrances in a similarly sturdy style.

Charity and Good Cheer

GOOD WORKS

'In 1781', wrote Barratt in his *Annals*, 'certain well-disposed Hampstead gentlemen formed themselves into an association with the kindly aim of detaching themselves from discord…and doing good service to the community.' What we might now call a sort of Rotarian Club, they called the Philo-Investigists, meaning lovers of investigation, and they addressed each other briefly as 'Brother Phil'.

The copper medallion *(79)* they produced for members shows an assortment of mystical symbols, including triangles, clouds, the sun and the moon, and the motto: 'Brother, do all the good you can.' The reverse has a picture of the Good Shepherd and his flock, with the injunction 'Feed my lambs', and the proud boast 'Sunday Schools Instituted 1787'. (One of these rare medallions can be seen at the Hampstead Museum in Burgh House.) Club members were enjoined 'to keep within the bounds of temperance' and in their conversation they were expected to introduce only 'topics that tend to improve the understanding and mend the heart'.

But apart from leading irreproachable lives, the Philo-Investigists took a positive step by founding the first Sunday School for the poor children of Hampstead, and directly from this institution grew our present Parochial School in Holly Bush Vale. The first master of the school, which began in 1790 with 120 pupils, was Thomas Mitchell, whose gravestone in the parish churchyard bears the club's triangular symbol.

After changing premises many times, girl pupils were accommodated in Abernethy House in Mount Vernon and, in 1856, the boys and infants were moved to a grand new building *(81)*, the nucleus of the present school. A Mission Hall was added in 1893 by Norman Shaw, the architect then living in Ellerdale Road, but this was refashioned in 1938 as the Moreland Hall.

In the 19th century Anglican schools, such as Hampstead Parochial, were known as National Schools, while nonconformist institutions were called British Schools. Of the latter the first in Hampstead was that in Heath Street, opened in 1862 next to the new Baptist Chapel. The impetus came from this neighbouring congregation, which itself had origin-

79 & 80. Philo-Investigists' Medallion, 1787. Obverse and reverse sides.

81. *Hampstead Parochial Schools*, architect's drawing by
W.G. and E. Habershon, c1855.

82. *Former Baptist Chapel* in Holly Mount, a photograph
published in Potter's *Random Recollections*, 1907.

ated in Holly Mount in 1818. Attendances at the
small chapel there grew steadily and, despite a splinter
group leaving to form the Ebenezer Strict Baptist
Chapel in New End, a larger building was needed by
the 1850s.

The older chapel was taken over by a printing
press in 1860 and so the *Hampstead and Highgate Express*,
still happily with us, was born. After 1883,
when the *Ham and High* moved down to the High
Street, the building was used by a rival paper, the
Hampstead Record; from 1911 it has been an artist's
studio.

Apart from the ministrations of the churches and
chapels of Hampstead, there were two local charities
which were devoted to the welfare of the poor. The
Wells Charity, already mentioned, was active in the
19th century, providing better accommodation for
the lower paid. In 1876, in a slummy area between
Heath Street and High Street, they erected a tene-

ment block, now called Wells Court. Though described in the 1960s, before Camden Council took it over, as 'grim-looking and sub-standard', the block was praised in its early days for its 'excellent sanitary arrangements and ventilation, occasioned by the staircase and passages being open to the air'. In 1880 the Wells Trust merged with another local charity, founded in 1642 by another manorial family, the Campdens, who gave fourteen acres of land at Child's Hill.

Among other benefactions the joint Wells and Campden Charity built in 1887 another tenement block in Holly Bush Vale (recently rebuilt as New Campden Court and taken over by Camden Council), and in 1888 the Flask Walk Baths, now converted to residential use. (There is no relation between the names Campden and Camden: the former has the same root as Chipping Campden and the latter as Camden Town)

83. *Wells Court, Oriel Place*, celebrating George V's coronation in 1910.

PROMINENT PUBS

Three old-established taverns of Hampstead have achieved fame far beyond the borough boundaries, largely because of their locations, their curious names and their appearance in song and story.

The Old Bull and Bush was a popular pub long before it was promoted by Florrie Forde in her music-hall song. Helped by its situation in the hamlet of North End, and at the entrance to Hampstead Heath, it was originally a farm house, which may explain the 'bull' in the title. It was said to be the first marital home of William Hogarth. The tavern developed in the early 18th century, and the 'bush' may derive from the wine bush, or ivy bush, which were recognised pub signs. Among other traditions, the artist Gainsborough may have caroused here with Reynolds and Garrick, and called it 'a delightful little snuggery'. Charles Dickens and George du Maurier were almost certainly regulars.

The title of Jack Straw's Castle has also been a problem for historians. The once popular theory was that Wat Tyler's lieutenant, Jack Straw, set up camp here in 1381 on his way to join the mainstream of the Peasants' Revolt. But all the evidence points in another direction – in fact, to Highbury, where Jack Straw may well have camped and where once stood another pub of the same name. 'Jack Straw' also once meant 'a countryman', just as 'Jack Tar' meant a sailor, and the Hampstead inn may well have chosen its name, first found in 1713, to indicate that it was in the country and on top of the world: it is undeniably the highest pub in London. Washington Irving wrote about Jack Straw's in his *Tales of a Traveller* in 1824. Dickens (again) invited his biographer, John Forster, to dine here in 1838, saying: 'I know of a good 'ouse, where we can have a red-hot chop and a glass of good wine.' Karl Marx and Friedrich Engels were frequent customers in the 1850s. Badly bombed in the last war Jack Straw's Castle was rebuilt in 1962 by Raymond Erith in a capriciously castellated style *(85)*.

Dickens appears yet again in the story of the Spaniards Inn *(86)*, which he made the setting for the arrest of Mrs Bardell in *The Pickwick Papers*. Various explanations have been put forward about the pub's name, mostly favouring the story that a Spanish Ambassador at the court of James I lived here and that his valet later opened the tavern. Astride the boundary with Barnet, the pub also controlled the entrance to the Bishop of London's park and exacted appropriate tolls. The 18th-century tollhouse has survived, unloved by motorists but restored by conservationists, who thereby won a Civic Trust Award in 1967. The inn, already mentioned in connection with Dick Turpin, improved its image in 1780. When some of the Gordon Rioters came this way to burn down Kenwood House, the landlord plied them with unlimited liquor until the military arrived to disperse the mob.

84. The Old Bull and Bush, a turn-of-the century postcard.

85. Jack Straw's Castle by T.H. Shepherd, 1834.

86. The Spaniards Inn, published by Dugdale, 1838.

Artists at Work

CONSTABLE

Many artists of note came to Hampstead in the 18th century, including Hogarth and Gainsborough, already mentioned, and George Romney, who built the studio house in Holly Bush Hill in 1797, now known as Romney's House. None of these stayed long nor, apparently, recorded the local scene.

John Constable, on the other hand, visited Hampstead over a period of fifteen years and painted the Heath, the houses, the trees and the clouds, and all aspects of local life. One of his earliest studies of Hampstead houses was of Admiral's House *(88)*, painted from the family's lodgings in Lower Terrace, where they stayed in the summers of 1821 and 1822. It was mainly for the health of his wife and children

87. *John Constable*, by Daniel Gardner, 1796.

88. *Admiral's House* by Constable, 1821.

89. *Work* by Ford Madox Brown, 1868.

that Constable first came here, and the whole family was so delighted with the scenery and the country air that they found a holiday home in Hampstead nearly every summer until 1827. In that year the artist took a house in Well Walk, which he kept until 1834. His wife, Maria, died there tragically young, and was the first of the family to be buried in the Parish Churchyard. Constable joined her there in 1837.

Admiral's House, built in 1700, is seen in our picture to have a flat roof with railings. This idea was introduced by a tenant who had been a naval lieutenant (not an admiral as once was thought), and who wanted his roof to look like the quarter-deck of a ship. He brought in several cannon, too, and fired them on royal birthdays and other celebratory occasions. The architect, Sir George Gilbert Scott, lived in this house from 1856–64. The small building in the left foreground of the picture was the home of the writer, John Galsworthy, between 1918 and 1933.

MADOX BROWN

Of all the Pre-Raphaelites and their circle, Ford Madox Brown was the most devoted to Hampstead, and his two major pictures painted here, *Work* and *An English Autumn Afternoon*, are accepted as two of his happiest achievements. *Work (89)*, which he began in 1852, was inspired by the sight of sewer-digging in The Mount, and the setting, with Heath Street on the right, is very recognisable. The artist wished to present an allegory of the different types of workers and the dignity of labour. The navvies in their 'manly and picturesque costume' are contrasted with the idle rich, behind them on horseback, and the idle poor, out-of-work haymakers lying beyond the railings. On the right are two brain-workers, identifiable as Thomas Carlyle (with hat) and F.D. Maurice, founder of the Working Men's College. Madox Brown drew his topographical details with great accuracy and worked on this picture and a replica for the next fifteen years: these are now in Birmingham and Manchester Art Galleries.

The Old Priory, Hampstead. 1869.

90. Old Frognal Priory, an 1869 view.

FROGNAL PRIORY

In mid-Victorian times artists flocked to Hampstead to sketch the picturesque ruins of Frognal Priory *(90)*, an architectural folly in lower Frognal, where no priory had ever stood. The mock-antique mansion originated about 1820 in the dream world of a retired public-house auctioneer, John Thompson, who incorporated any period features, real or fake, that he could acquire. The exterior was a riot of Tudor windows, Dutch gables and Norman battlements, and the interior furnishings and fittings were equally eclectic. The owner enjoyed showing his visitors Anne Boleyn's mirror, Cardinal Wolsey's sideboard and other antiques, and challenging them to say which were genuine and which not. The dilapidated property was demolished about 1880, and replaced with another remarkable house of the same name *(91)*.

This was commissioned by Edwin Tate, an executive of Tate & Lyle, from Norman Shaw in the same year (1885) that he designed an adjoining house for Kate Greenaway. The second Priory gave way in the 1930s to Frognal Close, of which the architect was E.L. Freud, son of Sigmund.

91. *New Frognal Priory*, designed by Norman Shaw, 1885.

STUDIOS

Colonies of artists settled in the lower Haverstock Hill area in the late 19th century. Steele's Studios, where C.R.W. Nevinson lived for many years, and Wychcombe Studios off England's Lane, where Arthur Rackham was active, still stand, but the studios of Parkhill Road have disappeared. First in the field, these were built about 1880 in what was then called Park Road; they were designed by T.K. Green, architect of many houses in Arkwright and Ellerdale Roads. Thomas Danby, the landscape artist, worked at no. 11.Parkhill Road in the 1870s, next door to where the sculptor, Henry Moore, lived in the 1930s. Moore was one of a group of distinguished artists who used the Mall Studios in the adjoining Tasker Road at this time. Others were Ben Nicholson and Barbara Hepworth, and together they made a significant contribution to the development of abstract art in this country.

92. *Studios* in Parkhill Road, *c*1880.

'Appy 'Ampstead

MORE RAILWAYS

After the stormy pioneering of the London North Western Railway near Primrose Hill there was a lull in local railroad building until 1860. In that year the Hampstead Junction Railway (otherwise Broad Street and North London Line nowadays) opened stations at Edgware Road, Finchley Road and Hampstead Heath.

The Finchley Road station (93), which was built amid fields well before that part of the new highway had been developed, originally had St John's Wood included in its title as a prestige symbol. By 1880, when it had become Finchley Road and Frognal, this station was joined by two others in the same road, servicing the Midland Railway (1868) and the Metropolitan and St John's Wood Railway (1879). The latter was joined by the Bakerloo Line in 1939 and the station rebuilt to allow for easy interchange. The Midland Railway linking Bedford and St Pancras (now familiarly known as the Bed-Pan line) had accomplished a remarkable engineering feat in building the mile-long Belsize Tunnel. Fortunately the

clay, dug out by hundreds of navvies, provided most of the twenty-two million bricks needed to line the tunnel.

The main victim of this concerted invasion of three railway systems was the village of West End. The lines criss-crossed each other in a great swathe of railroadery, so close to this peaceful community that the whole settlement was unsettled. The stately homes of West Hampstead closed down and their influential inhabitants left. The railways dug themselves in further, added more tracks and sidings and opened their three stations on West End Lane within a hundred yards of each other.

The busiest station on the Broad Street Line was undoubtedly Hampstead Heath, especially at weekends. Crowds of East Enders headed for the Heath, advertised as being only sixteen minutes from the City, and on Bank Holidays caused some chaos. Local residents were frequently harassed by holidaymakers demanding a drink of water, and were much relieved in 1881 when a Miss Crump erected a fountain on South End Green. At Easter 1892 a sudden shower drove crowds of visitors into the narrow entrance to the station and, in the ensuing panic, eight people were crushed to death and many injured. As Barratt reported: 'Immense numbers pressed forward to the staircase leading to the Up Platform and, being unable to force a passage

93. *Finchley Road & Frognal Station*, engraving from the *Illustrated London News*, 1860.

94. *North London (Broad Street) Line* poster, used soon after 1860.

95. *Hampstead Heath Station Disaster*, Easter Monday 1892, from the *Penny Illustrated Paper*.

because of the ticket-collector's box at the bottom, were thrown into such confusion that it was impossible for all to extricate themselves.' The station master told the inquest that some 30,000 adults and 8,000 juveniles had passed through the station that day.

'APPY 'AMPSTEAD

One of the long-standing attractions of Hampstead Heath had been the donkey rides. From the 1820s the parish council had debated 'the nuisance occasioned by the placing for hire of pony-chaises and donkies on the Heath', but it was not until 1871, when the Heath became public property, that the donkey touts were properly licensed and controlled. Mainly they operated at Whitestone Pond, which George du Maurier nicknamed 'Ponds Asinorum'. Donkey rides are still available here, but pony-chaises have long gone.

Other summertime haunts on the Heath were the Vale of Health pond, in popular parlance 'the Cockney Child's Seaside', and the various bathing ponds, no longer used for London's water supply.

In winter, then as now, the wild fowl took over the ponds and, in favourable conditions, tobogganers and others sported on the snowy slopes. George du Maurier's cartoon of high life on 'Les Montagnes de Hampstead' (100) includes his own St Bernard, Chang.

96. (Top right) Donkey rides near Whitestone Pond, by John Leech, 1860.

97. (Right) George du Maurier, from the Hampstead Annual 1897.

98. (Below) Children's Paddling Corner, Vale of Health, a turn-of-the century postcard.

677 HAMPSTEAD HEATH. — *Ladies Bathing.* — LL.

99. *Ladies Bathing* in the Heath pond, an Edwardian postcard.

100. *Les Montagnes de Hampstead* by George du Maurier, 1876.

The Broad Street Line was not the only cheap transport to the Heath. South End Green was also the terminus for trams and buses, and many came by horse-drawn vehicles. A popular music-hall song of the 1860s, *Hampstead is the place to ruralise (101)*, recounted a family's holiday visit to the Heath by horse van. Here they had many comical and tragical adventures, the worst being their tea in the Vale of Health where, as the picture shows, father found a large toad in the teapot.

The largest crowds came, of course, to the Bank Holiday Fairs, and it was then that the Heath was turned into 'Appy 'Ampstead. Small fairs had been organised in different parts of the parish since the 17th century. Apart from the West End Fair already mentioned, there were sporadic fairs in Flask Walk and a flurry of sideshows round South End Green. In the 1830s the manorial Heathkeeper was authorised to suppress stalls and swings on the Green, but from 1860 the railway crowds created an ever-growing demand for sideshows and the Lord of the Manor decided to cash in instead. In about 1865, when an estimated 50,000 people visited the Heath at Easter, Sir Thomas Maryon Wilson designated part of the Lower Heath as a fairground and rented out pitches for stalls. swings and roundabouts.

LES MONTAGNES DE HAMPSTEAD.

SHOWING HOW WE ADVENTUROUS INHABITANTS OF THE HILLY SUBURBS OF NORTH LONDON BEGUILED THE WEARY HOURS RECENT SNOWY WEATHER.

101. *Hampstead is the Place to Ruralise* sheet-music cover, drawn by R.J. Hamerton, *c*1863.

A panoramic picture of *Hampstead Heath on Whit Monday (103)* appeared in the *Illustrated London News* in 1872, the year after the Bank Holiday Act had created the Easter, Whit and August Bank Holiday Mondays. This shows a lively scene on the slopes behind the Vale of Health, with a rather well-dressed crowd in the foreground and a number of coconut shies and other sports and games in the rear. At the back of the picture, near the flagstaff by Whitestone Pond, can be seen some diminutive donkey riders. Of historical interest is (top left) the spire of Christ Church under construction, twenty years after the body of the church was built.

The cockneys and costers took Hampstead into their hearts and into their rhyming slang.'Hampstead Heath', or just ''Ampsteads', means teeth.

102.'Appy 'Arriet at 'Ampstead, late Victorian postcard from the Hugh Curtis Collection.

103. Hampstead Heath on a holiday from the *Illustrated London News*, 1872.

VALE OF HEALTH

Apart from South End Green, the area most affected by the new holiday crowds was the Vale of Health. Originating only in 1777, when the source of the River Fleet was dammed to form a reservoir and the surrounding swamp drained, the Vale had already survived a cockney invasion in Regency times. But that was the arrival of Leigh Hunt and his so-called Cockney Poets, the like of Keats, who thereupon fell in love with Hampstead, and Shelley, who amused Hunt's many children by sailing paper-boats on the pond. In mid-Victorian times the Vale was noted for its colony of laundresses and a few rickety tea-gardens but, after 1860, refreshments of all sorts were in greater demand and the vast Hampstead Heath Hotel was built beside the pond to cater for the crowds.

The Suburban Hotel Company's promotional picture *(104)* shows the hotel's terraces, turrets and grottoes, and boating on the pond, which was soon prohibited after a drowning accident. On the left are seen the Villas on the Heath. Described at its opening

104. The Hampstead Heath Hotel built in the Vale of Health in 1863, a lithograph by F. Waller.

THE SUBURBAN HOTEL COMPANY LIMITED.

A SKETCH OF THEIR FIRST HOTEL RECENTLY ERECTED IN THE VALE OF HEALTH IN THE CENTRE OF HAMPSTEAD HEATH.

105. Stanley Spencer painting the Vale of Health mat-slide in the 1920s (photograph by J.B. Rustomjee).

in 1863 as a 'palatial establishment which has elicited universal public admiration, both for its beautiful castellated style and its admirable internal arrangements', this pretentious hostelry offered extensive tea gardens and smoking cabins, and was also 'providing for the comfort of the working classes, for whose convenience there is a commodious taproom, together with enclosed bowling alleys'. Despite all these facilities the hotel thrived only during the short summer seasons and had to close within five years. After brief periods as a factory, a restaurant and a Salvation Army barracks, the building became the more modest Vale of Health Tavern in the early 20th century, with a large studio on the top floor.

The artist, Henry Lamb, used the studio from 1912 to 1924, and was succeeded by Stanley Spencer, who completed his famous *Cookham Resurrection* here. The picture, now in the Tate Gallery, could only be taken out of the studio by removing one of the windows. The artist was commemorated in the block of flats, Spencer House, which replaced the tavern in 1967.

Writers as well as artists have frequented the Vale in this century, notably D.H. Lawrence, Compton Mackenzie and Edgar Wallace. Lawrence came in 1915, and here witnessed a Zeppelin raid on London, which he described in his novel *Kangaroo*.

A curious, chapel-like building called the Athenaeum was erected near the hotel, also in the 1860s. There is no record of its being used for any religious purpose, except from 1882 when part of it was let to the Salvation Army. Curiously, the lessor and main occupant was the Anglo-German Club, whose riotous presence in the Vale was the chief object of the local Army's displeasure. Salvation was not achieved and the Army retreated in 1886. The bonfire on the adjoining heath that year, doubtless supported by victorious club members, burned an effigy not of Guy Fawkes but of a Salvation Army Commandant.

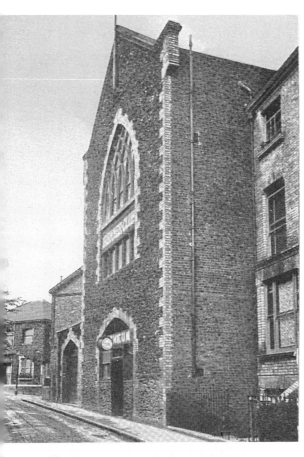

106. The Athenaeum, an undated postcard of the Anglo-German Club's base in the Vale of Health.

107. Building the bonfire on the Heath for November 5, using barrels of pitch. (From the *Daily Graphic*, 1907)

1866 and All That

ORDNANCE SURVEY

The first detailed and reliable map of Hampstead was the result of an ordnance survey in 1866 by Captain the Hon. W. Trench, engraved under the direction of Colonel Cameron and published in 1870 by Major General James. The picture the map presents is of a small town surrounded by heath and meadows, except in the south, where Haverstock Hill links up with London's northern suburbs. North End, West End and South End Green are still separate from the main town.

A look at the centre section (108) finds the High Street as wide as it is now, except in its northern stretch, which was to be opened out in the 1880s. At that time Heath Street was to be extended to the

south west from the Police Station to meet Fitzjohns Avenue. Two important buildings named in New End are the Workhouse, later to become the hospital, and the Provident Dispensary, erected in 1853 to provide cheap medicine and soup for the needy.

Not named in New End Square is Burgh House; this is part of the cluster of buildings labelled Militia Barracks. A French invasion scare in 1852 had prompted the formation of 'territorial' regiments all over the country and Hampstead became the headquarters of the Royal East Middlesex Militia. Burgh House was taken over from the Burgh family as an Officers' Mess, and extra barracks were built on either side of the parade ground created in the front garden. (These blocks can be seen in the photograph and the map.) Married quarters for sergeants and bandsmen were added in Willow Road in 1863 – the latter blocks still stand in much altered form under the name Willow Hall. Proposals to upgrade Hampstead to a brigade headquarters were resisted by residents in 1881 and the Militia departed.

108. *Ordnance Survey map* of central Hampstead, 1866.

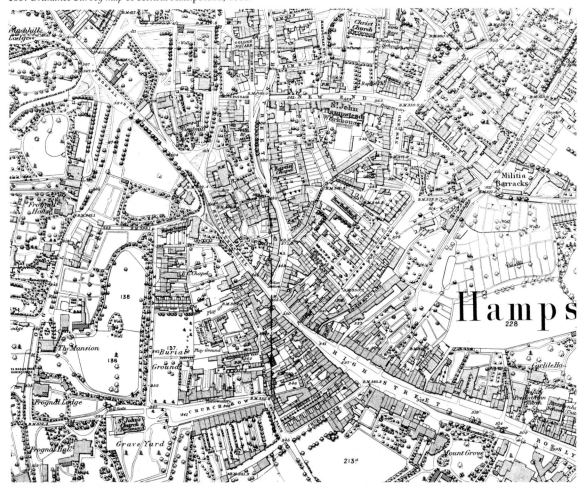

109. *Burgh House* as Militia Headquarters, seen from across Well Walk, c1870.

110. *Willow Hall*, drawn by Sydney Arrobus, 1960s.

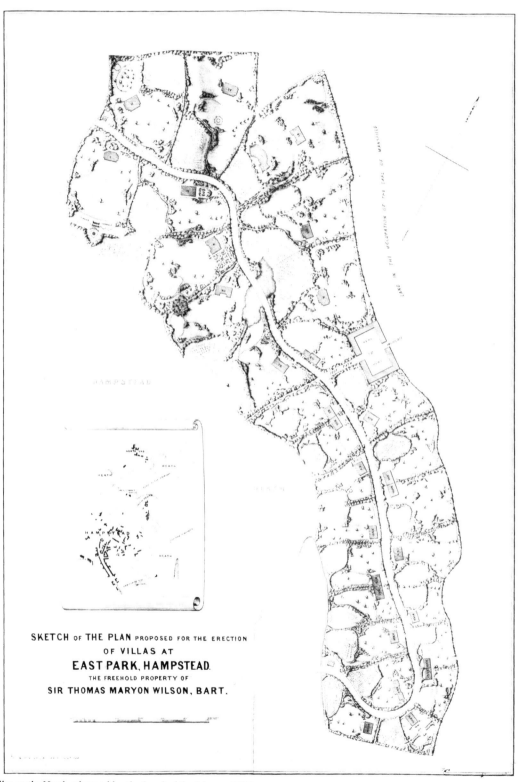

SKETCH of THE PLAN PROPOSED FOR THE ERECTION
OF VILLAS AT
EAST PARK, HAMPSTEAD.
THE FREEHOLD PROPERTY OF
SIR THOMAS MARYON WILSON, BART.

111. *Villas on the Heath,* planned by the Lord of the Manor, 1844.

South of the barracks on the map can be seen the town allotments, which were developed into Gayton Road and Crescent by 1870. South again is the Carlile House estate which was also built up a few years later. The principal street was named Willoughby Road after Mr Carlile's solicitor and son-in-law.

HEATH AND HILL

Of two wars that were waged in Hampstead in the late 1860s, that to preserve the Heath for the public was by far the fiercest. Since 1829 Sir Thomas Maryon Wilson, Lord of the Manor of Hampstead, had been trying in vain to obtain a Private Act of Parliament to enable him to build on the Heath. In 1844, as a defiant gesture, he drew up plans for luxury villas on the East Park Estate, now part of the East Heath, and laid down a road from Jack Straw's Castle to Downshire Hill, including the Viaduct Bridge, which is still a picturesque feature on the Heath.

Later, he began demonstrating his rights over the Heath by charging rents to casual users, even to washerwomen with their laundry, and by digging out sand to sell to builders. Up to thirty loads of sand per day were removed in the 1860s, a rate of excavation that altered the contours of the Heath quite dramatically. In 1866, having claimed that he owned the Heath 'upwards to heaven and downwards to the centre of the earth', he decided to assert his building rights by erecting a house on the Heath near Whitestone Pond.

This spurred the local opposition, headed by the banker, John Gurney Hoare, into immediate legal action in Chancery to challenge Wilson's rights. Proceedings dragged on until 1869 when, as a local councillor commented, 'the hopes of Hampstead people were brightened by the death of Sir Thomas'. His heir, Sir John, was more amenable to negotiation. The Lord's manorial rights were acquired in 1871 for £45,000, and the Heath – much smaller than we know today – was saved.

112. Sand-digging on Sandy Heath, with Spaniards Road behind, a photograph used in the Chancery proceedings of 1867.

Meanwhile, a smaller battle in Belsize Park had been lost. Sir Rowland Hill, originator of the Penny Post in 1840, had strongly opposed the siting of a smallpox hospital behind his house on Hampstead Green, not only objecting to the intrusion on his privacy, but rightly pointing out that local residents might be infected by the disease. Nevertheless a temporary hospital was built here and by 1874 was pressing for expansion. Sir Rowland again led the protesters, who included local landowners concerned at the 'ruinous depreciation of valuable property'. But plans for the North Western Fever Hospital went ahead and, when Sir Rowland died in 1879, his house was bought up and built on by the hospital. Following the Fever Hospital came the much larger Hampstead General Hospital in 1906 and, on the same site, the mighty Royal Free in 1969.

113. *Sir Rowland Hill* (1795–1879).

114. *Bartram House*, home of Sir Rowland Hill, watercolour by Mary Ann Baily, 1901.

115. *Advertisement* for Belsize Park cowkeeper and dairyman, 1860s.

116. *The Boys' Home and Industrial School* at the corner of King Henry's Road and Regent's Park Road. The school, which moved here in 1865, was aimed at 'the Maintenance by their own Labour of Destitute Boys not Convicted of Crime'. This wood engraving was on the cover of their magazine in 1883.

Improvements

Among the first houses were a number of prestigious ones designed by prominent architects for fashionable artists. Norman Shaw, for example, contributed Three Gables for the portrait painter Frank Holl. (The Tavistock Clinic now stand on its site.) Several artists would open their studios to the public on a 'Show Sunday' and attract the smart set to what Barratt called 'this commanding, tree-beautified avenue of stately dwellings'. The prevailing architectural style was Queen Anne Revival which was, Barratt added, 'considered very wonderful by a generation accustomed to the frowning dinginess of Georgian bricks and mortar'.

Many of the rather eccentric Victorian houses here were built with bricks made on the Heath near the Viaduct Bridge. This part of the East Park Estate had been leased to a local builder in about 1865 for twenty-one years, and during that time, according to a report in the *Illustrated London News*, had been 'chopped and carved in a manner utterly destructive of its natural form, which was that of a hill gracefully swelling with a fine outline'.

FITZJOHNS AVENUE

In 1875 Sir John Maryon Wilson, the new Lord of the Manor of Hampstead, sold fifty acres of his farmland to developers for £50,000. This allowed the building of a·major new thoroughfare to connect Swiss Cottage and central Hampstead. It was called Fitzjohns Avenue after a Maryon Wilson estate in Essex.

117. *Three Gables, Fitzjohns Avenue* by Norman Shaw, 1881 (photographed 1951).

118. Brickfields on East Park Estate, *c*1880.

TOWN IMPROVEMENTS

When Fitzjohns Avenue reached the top of the hill in the late 1870s it had practically nowhere to go. As the 1866 map shows, the centre of Hampstead between Church Row and the High Street was a jumble of alleys and courtyards, quite unsuitable for through traffic. The narrow Church Place led from Church (now Perrins) Lane to Oriel House, which faced down Church Row. (Oriel House, with its two-storey bay, has left its name on two local streets.)

North of Church Place the road narrowed even further into Little Church Row, a dilapidated alleyway, on which was a Primitive Methodist Chapel, and off which there were several crumbling courtyards. The largest of these was Yorkshire Grey Yard (site of the Express Dairy building), which surrounded the ancient Yorkshire Grey inn, used sometimes for civic matters such as inquests. It was also the popular haunt of the Irish navvies building the local railways.

Further north the pathway forked into two decrepit alleys called Bradleys Buildings. Of these the left prong followed the line of the present Holly Bush Vale, and an 1880s watercolour *(121)* shows the houses on the site of the Everyman Cinema. The ornate doorway depicted led to the Hampstead Parochial Schools.

119. Church Place from a watercolour by G.C. Maund, 1877.

120. *Little Church Row,* an anonymous watercolour of the 1880s.

After seven years debate it was decided to cut through these slum areas and link Fitzjohns Avenue with Heath Street. As the terraces on the west side of Holly Hill then continued unbroken into the High Street, several houses and shops had to be demolished, which is why now there are no nos. 51–54 High Street.

Apart from extending Heath Street to achieve this, it was agreed to widen the northern part of the High Street which, above Perrins Court, narrowed to about fifteen feet. All the houses on the west side above no. 70 were accordingly demolished together with the slums behind. Three pubs were included in the destruction but one of them, the Three Horseshoes, was rebuilt in Heath Street.

The Improvements, which cost £120,000, were declared complete in February 1888. The scheme cost £120,000; half was paid by Hampstead Vestry and half by the Metropolitan Board of Works, the forerunner of the London County Council. It was the biggest upheaval in Hampstead's urban history and, needless to say, not everyone was happy with this drastic surgery. As the *Daily Graphic* commented: 'Town Improvements have swept away many of the interesting relics of Hampstead's picturesque past.'

121. *Bradley's Buildings*, watercolour by F. Calvert, 1886.

122. *Hampstead High Street*, west side, by J.P. Emslie, 1882.

123. *Nos. 65–68 Hampstead High Street*, c1885, preparing for the Town Improvements: 'To effect an immediate sale, a great sacrifice will be made'.

ECCLESIASTICAL

The building of Christ Church in 1852 was an early attempt to accommodate Hampstead's growing Anglican congregation and the formation of this new parish was the first inroad into the wide-ranging territory of the old parish church. St Saviour's, Eton Road (1856), St Peter's, Belsize Park (1859), and St Mary's, Abbey Road, (1862), followed. In the 1860s there was special concern among the residents in the Finchley Road area for the souls of the railway navvies who were active in the neighbourhood. A mission hall was erected in Belsize Lane, and a pastor was found in the shape of the Rev. Henry Sharpe, recently returned from the Canadian backwoods.

124. *Mission Hall and School* in Belsize Lane, 1875.

Among his pastoral activities he would visit the Belsize Tunnel and preach to his flock sixty feet underground. The more permanent congregation which supported this venture was able to raise funds to build Holy Trinity Church in Finchley Road in 1872, which was replaced a century later by a smaller church.

Meanwhile, in 1869, a more imposing church, St Stephen's, had sprung up at the corner of Rosslyn Hill and Pond Street, on a triangular piece of manorial wasteland riddled with streams. S.S. Teulon, the architect, overcame this difficulty by building the church on arches and, with its fanciful French Gothic interior, St Stephen's was considered to be his masterpiece. He died, exhausted, soon after its completion. In the 1880s over 1300 people attended a Sunday service here, but by 1902 the figure was down to 540. The church was made redundant in 1977.

Other sizeable Anglican churches built in the Victorian era were All Souls, Loudon Road (1865), St Mary the Virgin, Primrose Hill (1867), St Cuthbert's, Fordwych Road (1887), St James's, West End Lane (1888), St Luke's, Kidderpore Avenue (1896), and Emmanuel, West End Green (1897).

Nonconformist groups were also active. Unitarians were already established on Rosslyn Hill, Roman Catholics were in Holly Place and the Baptists were in Heath Street. The Presbyterians, who had rented the Temperance Hall in Perrins Court in the 1840s and the old Long Room in Well Walk in the 1850s, finally built a grand chapel in Willoughby Road in 1862. Exactly a hundred years later its congregation moved out to St Andrew's, Frognal Lane, and most of the old building was demolished; the church hall was converted into the present Trinity Close.

Also in the 1860s, Quex Road in West Hampstead became the scene of much ecclesiastical actitvity. Among the meadows of Kilburn, a temporary building for the Roman Catholic Church of the Sacred Heart in 1868 was joined the following year by a Wesleyan Chapel and a Unitarian Church. The main Congregational church was the hexagonal building in Lyndhurst Road (1884) by Alfred Waterhouse. Its congregation, too, migrated to St Andrew's where the United Reform Church now flourishes.

125. *Samuel Sanders Teulon* (1812–73), an RIBA photograph.

126. *Trinity Church, Willoughby Road*, erected 1862.

127. St Stephen's, Rosslyn Hill, by S.S. Teulon, 1869.

128. Congregational Church, Lyndhurst Road, by Alfred Waterhouse, 1884.

EDUCATIONAL

'Hampstead Board Schools are amongst the most successful in the metropolis', commented a contributor to Baines's *Records of Hampstead*, published in 1890. By then the London School Board had founded schools at the foot of Haverstock Hill and in Netherwood Street, Kilburn, both housing one thousand children, and smaller establishments in Broomsleigh Street, off Mill Lane, and in Fleet Road.

The last-named began in great difficulties in a notoriously unhealthy area, menaced by the dust from the local brickfields and the Carpet Beating Ground, damp from the River Fleet, and possible disease from the North Western Fever Hospital. Nevertheless, Fleet Road Primary prospered and grew, at one stage accommodating 1700 pupils, and won a remarkable number of scholarships to secondary schools. It was soon known as the Harrow (or Eton) of the Board Schools. Of the National (Anglican) Schools flourishing in late Victorian times, Hampstead Parochial was the oldest and largest, followed by Christ Church, founded in 1855. There

were also small church schools, such as the one in Downshire Hill from the 1830s.

The only British (Nonconformist) Schools were attached to the Unitarian and Baptist Chapels, but in 1900 the latter, with its 374 scholars, was taken over by the London School Board, and after six years was rehoused in the towering block of New End School, designed by T.J. Bailey and built with some ingenuity over a source of the River Fleet.

In his *Hampstead, Building a Borough*, F.M.L. Thompson noted that many of the large family residences built in Hampstead in the 1890s proved difficult to let or sell, and that in them 'a rash of discreet girls' schools broke out'. By this time South Hampstead High School for Girls had already opened in Winchester Road in 1876 and it re-opened in Maresfield Gardens six years later. Not long after, its first headmistress left to found a rival establishment in Belsize Park, taking many of her pupils with her. The breakaway was successful, and she was able to build what is now the Hall School in Crossfield Road in 1890. It was most unfortunate for the new school that, in that very year, a Kentish Town nursemaid

129. Fleet Road School, cookery class, c1907.

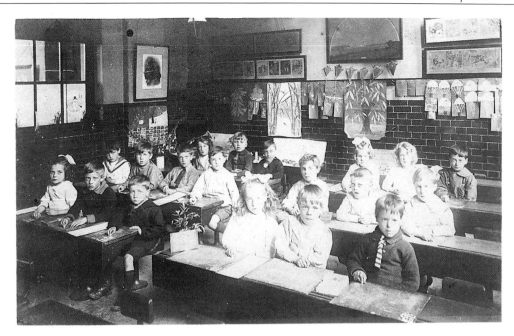

130. *New End School,* c1920.

131. *South Hampstead High School* in the days of gymslips.

132. *The Hall School's hall*, an 1894 photograph.

133. *Haberdashers' Aske's School*, Westbere Road, an Edwardian postcard.

called Mrs Pearcey should have murdered her mistress and dumped the corpse in Crossfield Road. The murder was soon the talk of the town and Mrs Pearcey, though quickly tried and hanged, achieved lasting fame in Tussaud's Chamber of Horrors. The Hall School overcame this drama, but in 1905 it became a boys' school, which is now celebrating its centenary.

Among the many private schools that set up in Hampstead at the turn of the century, two were long-established foundations. The Haberdashers' Aske's school in the City of London came out to the fresh air of Westbere Road in 1898. In 1961 it sought even fresher air and moved to Elstree and their old building became the Hampstead Comprehensive. University College School, begun in 1830 in Gower Street, moved in 1907 to Hampstead, where its present impressive building, designed by Arnold Mitchell and opened by Edward VII, dominates the slopes of Frognal.

134. *UCS Junior School*, Holly Hill, a pre–1928 postcard.

135. *King Edward VII opening UCS Senior School*, Frognal, 1907.

Public Works

BIRTH OF A BOROUGH

The rapid growth of Hampstead in the second half of the 19th century created a demand for a bigger parish council, called the Vestry, and for capacious offices to house it and its staff. Vestrymen had hitherto met in cramped quarters at the workhouse, but in 1878 they built their Town Hall in Haverstock Hill. The Italianate style was then in fashion and the building was widely admired, but it did not find favour with Nikolaus Pevsner, who dismissed it in the 1950s as 'crushingly mean; a disgrace to so prosperous and artistic a borough'.

In 1885 Hampstead had its first chance to elect its own representative to Parliament and it chose a Conservative, Sir Henry Holland. Three years later, with the formation of the London County Council, the parish officially ceased to be in Middlesex and became part of London. With such greatness thrust upon it the Vestry decided to abandon its old emblem of a sprig of holly and to choose a municipal coat of arms. The result was an ingenious amalgam of the Arms of some of the more significant Lords of the Manor of Hampstead. Westminster Abbey was represented by the mitre, Lord Campden by the fleur-de-lys, and the Gainsborough family by lattice work. The crest of a buck's head derived from both the Campdens and Gainsboroughs, and the holly wreath around its neck was a reminder of Hampstead's humbler origins. After toying with an all-or-nothing French motto, *Tout bien ou rien*, the Council opted for a public-spirited Latin flourish meaning 'Not for self but for all'.

In 1900 the Vestry was replaced by Hampstead Borough Council, which elected Sir Henry Harben, the locally benevolent chairman of the Prudential Assurance Company, as its first mayor. The Borough, preserving the almost identical parish boundaries that were outlined in Anglo-Saxon charters, survived until its absorption into Camden in 1965.

136. *Coat of Arms of Hampstead Vestry (later Borough)*, adopted in 1897.

137. *Sir Henry Harben*, the first Mayor of Hampstead in 1900.

POLICE

When Sir Robert Peel reorganised the police force in 1830, Hampstead Vestry protested at the imposition of Peelers on its own area. 'There is not wanted more vigilance than our former system of Watching produced,' and 'we are not exposed to depredations.' More importantly the new police would 'increase our burthen of taxation by upwards of eleven hundred pounds per annum'. Nevertheless, the Peelers moved in promptly, closing down the local lock-ups in Cannon Lane and the old Watch House on Flask Walk Green, where the village stocks reputedly stood.

After four years at no. 9 Holly Walk, the new police moved in 1834 to better premises at the foot of Holly Hill, and again in 1868 to a new building on the *west* side of Rosslyn Hill. Continuing their progress downhill, the force finally took over their present premises at the corner of Downshire Hill in 1913. Designed by J.D. Butler, a disciple of Norman Shaw, the building was given modified praise by Pevsner as 'oversize but very pretty'.

138. Police Station (left), in Rosslyn Hill, opened in 1868.

FIRE

Until the 1850s fire-fighting in Hampstead was a haphazard business. The Vestry did little but provide a rather primitive pump-engine at a High Street tavern or next to the police station, and so, many houses relied instead on the fire brigade organised by the leading fire insurers. The plaques of some of those companies, together with the policy numbers of the residents, may still be seen on walls of local houses.

The Metropolitan Fire Brigade, formed in 1856, established its first station in Hampstead in 1869, near the George Inn on Haverstock Hill. But four years later operations were transferred to the grand new building at the corner of Holly Hill and Heath Street, opposite today's Underground station. This fire station had stables for the horses on the ground floor, mechanical devices for the rapid lowering of saddles onto their backs, and a wide doorway to allow engines to dash out. An upper floor contained quarters for the firemen, in the tower was a water tank and, a little later, a not very reliable clock bought by public subscription. The topmost observation post (since removed) was used for firewatching in two World Wars though by 1915 the Fire Brigade had moved down to Lancaster Grove.

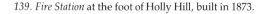

139. Fire Station at the foot of Holly Hill, built in 1873.

Fire Station, Hampstead.

140. Fire Engine racing down the High Street, a turn-of-the-century photograph by Arthur Knowles Brown, the local jeweller.

LIBRARIES

In 1833 the Hampstead Public Library of General Literature and Elementary Science was established by public subscription at no. 65 Flask Walk. John Constable, then living in Well Walk, was among the founder members. Over the years, as the library changed premises and finally settled in Stanfield House in 1885, its elitist membership became more charitable and offered a reading room and a free lending service for the working classes; also provided was a side door to the library so that the underprivileged readers need not be seen in receipt of charity.

It was not until 1892 that the local council provided a free library service, first in an adapted house at no. 48 Priory Road and, five years later, in a custom-built library in Antrim Road. Its ceremonial opening was delayed a year by a strike and its closure came ignominiously soon, in 1936, when so many design defects had been found that complete reconstruction was necessary. The present building was opened in 1937.

The Council's Central Library was housed in a Tudor-style building in Arkwright Road (now Camden Arts Centre) from 1897, and transferred to Swiss Cottage in 1964, the year after the original Subscription Library had finally closed.

141. Antrim Road Library; Vestrymen laying the foundation stone in 1896.

ELECTRICITY

Rejecting many offers of privatisation, Hampstead was the second borough in London to establish its own electricity supply. Taking over the old Stone Yard in the suitably named Lithos Road, the Council built its power station there in 1894 to serve both private and public lighting. Though never the money-maker its builders had hoped for the municipal supply was immediately in great demand by rich and poor. 'It may be presumed', said a trade paper of the time, 'that the wealthy of Hampstead will enjoy the luxury of electric lighting and that the artistic element in the population will welcome it in preference to gas.'

142. Staff outing from the Lithos Road electricity station, c1900.

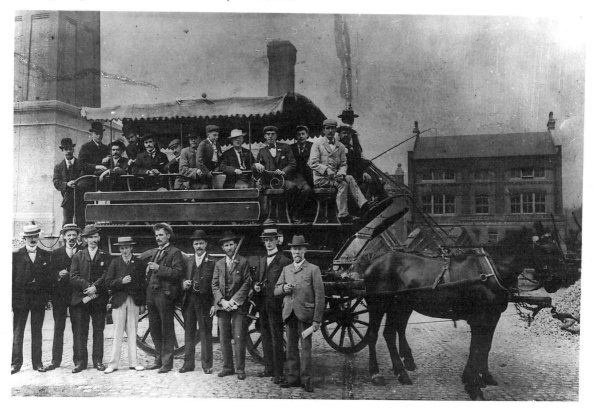

Late Victorians

HEALTH

In 1856 Hampstead Vestry appointed Dr Charles Lord as its first Medical Officer of Health; his duties included those of Sanitary Inspector, Public Vaccinator and Workhouse Doctor. During his service of twenty-three years Lord saw the completion of the local sewerage system, the opening of Hampstead's first cemetery at Fortune Green, and the constant cleansing, flushing-out and lime-washing of stables, cowsheds and, above all, slaughter houses. But, as Thompson reported, 'Pigs had been his greatest enemies, associated as they were with poverty, filth and disease, and the obstinate refusal of their owners to part with them.'

Hampstead still had the reputation of being the healthiest place in London, and soon after the opening of Smallpox and Fever Hospitals in Belsize Park came the massive Consumption Hospital in 1880. This establishment, which had small beginnings in an outpatients' dispensary in Tottenham Court Road, lodged briefly at Stanfield House while the new hospital for over a hundred in-patients was built on Mount Vernon. Unfortunately neither the original pseudo-chateau by Roger Smith, nor the western extension by Maxwell Ayrton, really suited their surroundings. The hospital migrated to Mill Hill before World War I and is now in Northwood, but still with Mount Vernon in its name. Meanwhile the building was taken over as a National Institute, first for Medical Research and latterly for Biological Standards and Control. At the time of writing the premises are vacant and ripe for redevelopment.

143. Butcher's Advertisement, including picture of his slaughterhouse at the back of England's Lane, 1880s.

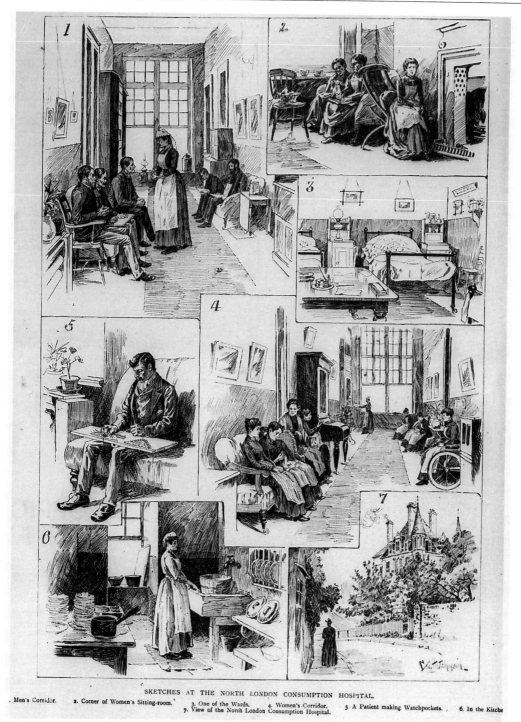

SKETCHES AT THE NORTH LONDON CONSUMPTION HOSPITAL.

Men's Corridor.   2. Corner of Women's Sitting-room.   3. One of the Wards.   4. Women's Corridor.   5 A Patient making Watchpockets.   6. In the Kitche
7. View of the North London Consumption Hospital.

144. *Mount Vernon Hospital,* drawn by George Hutchinson, c1880.

PUBS

Many of the public houses of Hampstead began as beer shops, selling through the front windows of their parlours. The Old Black Lion in West End Lane was a licensed beerhouse in 1721, but it was not until the end of the 19th century that it became a fully-fledged tavern with snuggeries inside and shelters on its forecourt. It was rebuilt in 1912 and has been enlarged and modernised since.

The fate of the City Arms in New End was quite different. Popular as a pub in the 1850s, it was reduced to beer retailing in late Victorian times and by 1910 had been closed and taken over for use as a school house by New End School. The picture *(146)* shows the lower slopes of New End in 1880, with the erstwhile City Arms on the left, now W. Taylor's beer shop – the pub sign is clearly missing. At the top of the slope is the large Provident Dispensary, erected in 1853 from voluntary contributions as a thank-offering for the parish being spared from a London cholera epidemic. This dispensary, which lasted for nearly a century, is now a private school. Across the road from here is Ye Olde White Bear, which dates back to 1704, and whose success may have hastened the City Arms' decline.

145. *The Old Black Lion*, West End Lane, from a watercolour by J.T. Wilson, 1896.

146. *New End* with the former City Arms (left), by J.P. Emslie, 1880.

147. *Ye Olde White Bear*, New End, *c*1904.

SOUTH HAMPSTEAD ADVERTISER

Circulated GRATUITOUSLY to every House in the District.

No. 1. WEDNESDAY, DECEMBER 1st, 1880. **2000 copies Gratis.**

Issued from Baines's Printing Offices, 79, Fairfax Road, South Hampstead.

S. S. SMALLWOOD,
Milliner & Fancy Draper
75, Fairfax Road,
Opposite Loudoun Road Station.

R. H. MIZEN,
COOK & CONFECTIONER,
55, FAIRFAX ROAD.

Wedding Breakfasts, Dinners, and Ball Suppers supplied Soups, Entreés, Ices, Jellies

S. KITE,
Furnishing & General Ironmonger
Gasfitter, Bell-hanger, and Locksmith,
81, FAIRFAX ROAD, N.W.

Rout Seats, Glass, Cutlery, and Plate lent on Hire.

Fairfax Road, near Swiss Cottage,
YEO,
FISHMONGER
AND
ICE MERCHANT.

ALFRED GOSS,
TAILOR, &c.,
(From Conduit Street, W.)
1, Blenheim Terrace, Abbey Road,
The best Goods, Style, and Workmanship at moderate prices.

Orders by Post punctually attended to.

Established 22 Years.

R. BRIGHTWELL,
FAMILY BUTCHER
6, Swiss Terrace, Belsize Road,
AND
99, Henry Street, St. John's Wood.

Meat of the best quality supplied at the lowest possible prices.

BEEF.	d.	MUTTON.	s.	d.
Ribs & Sirloin...	10½	Legs............	0	10½
Aitch Bones......	7	Haunches......	0	10½
Beefs..............	11	Shoulders	0	9
Veal Fillets	11	Saddles	0	10½
Necks & Breasts.	8	Necks	0	8½
Shoulders.........	8	Chops	1	0
		PORK.		
		Legs large ...	0	8½
		Loins..	0	9

Orders by Post sent by the first delivery.

LONDON & NORTH WESTERN RAILWAY.

Up Trains.	a.m.	a.m.	a.m.	a.m.	a.m.	a.m.	a.m.	a.m.	a.m.	a.m.	a.m.	a.m.	a.m.	a.m.	a.m.	a.m.	noon
WILLESDEN ..	7 49	8 10	8 10	8 24	8 28	8 34	8 46	8 56	9 10	9 30	9 34	9 50	1034	1056	1134	1156	1234
KILBURN .	7 54	8 15	8 17	8 29	8 35	8 39	8 52	9 3	9 16	9 35	9 39	9 56	1039	11 3	1139	12 3	1239
LOUDOUN ROAD	**7 56**	**8 17**	**8 20**	**8 32**	**8 38**	**8 41**	**8 55**	**9 6**	**9 18**	**9 38**	**9 41**	**9 58**	**1041**	**11 6**	**1141**	**12 6**	**1241**
BROAD STREET	8 21	8 35		8 50		9 6	9 14		9 35		10 6	1018	11 6		12 6		1 6
EUSTON			8 30	X	8 48			9 15	X	9 47		X		1117		1220	

continued—	noon	p.m.	p.m.	*	p.m.	p.m.	*	p.m.	p.m.	†	p.m.	p.m.	†	p.m.	p.m.	†	p.m.
WILLESDEN ...	1256	1 34	1 56	2 4	2 34	2 56	3 4	3 34	3 56	4 0	4 34	4 56	5 23	5 34	5 56	6 4	6 34
KILBURN	1 3	1 39	2 3	2 9	2 39	3 3	3 9	3 39	4 3	4 7	4 39	5 3	5 28	5 39	6 3	6 9	6 39
LOUDOUN ROAD	**1 6**	**1 41**	**2 6**	**2 11**	**2 41**	**3 6**	**3 11**	**3 41**	**4 6**	**4 10**	**4 41**	**5 6**	**5 31**	**5 41**	**6 6**	**6 11**	**6 41**
BROAD STREET		2 6		2 36	3 6		3 36	4 6		4 30	5 6		5 50	6 6		6 36	7 6
EUSTON ...	1 15		2 20			3 20			4 15			5 15			6 15		

continued—	p.m.	p.m.	†	p.m.	p.m.	p.m.	p.m.	p.m.	p.m.	p.m.	p.m.	p.m.	SUNDAYS. a.m.	p.m.	p.m.	p.m.
WILLESDEN	6 50	6 56	7 4	7 34	7 56	8 4	8 34	8 56	9 34	9 56	1034	1119	9 10	1 25	7 43	9 36
KILBURN	6 55	7 3	7 9	7 39	8 3	8 9	8 39	9 3	9 39	10 3	1039	1124	9 23	1 34	7 51	9 43
LOUDOUN ROAD	**6 57**	**7 6**	**7 11**	**7 41**	**8 6**	**8 11**	**8 41**	**9 6**	**9 41**	**10 6**	**1041**	**1126**	**9 26**	**1 38**	**7 55**	**9 46**
BROAD STREET	7 17		7 36	8 6		8 36	9 6		10 6		11 6	1151				
EUSTON ...		7 15			8 15			9 15		1015			9 40	1 50	8 10	10 0

Down Trains	a.m.	a.m.	a.m.	a.m.	a.m.	a.m.	a.m.	a.m.	a.m.	a.m.	a.m.	a.m.	a.m.	a.m.	noon	noon	p.m.
EUSTON			8 35							1035	†		1135		1235		*
BROAD STREET	6 45	7 45			8 45	9 8	9 35	9 45	10 5		1035	1045		1145		1245	1 15
LOUDOUN ROAD	**7 14**	**8 14**	**8 44**	**8 55**	**9 14**	**9 25**	**9 55**	**1014**		**1044**	**1054**	**1114**	**1144**	**1214**	**1244**	**1 14**	**1 44**
KILBURN	7 16	8 16	8 47	8 57	9 16	9 28	9 58	1016	1029	1047	1057	1116	1147	1216	1247	1 16	1 46
WILLESDEN	7 21	8 21	8 53	9 2	9 21	9 33	10 3	1021	1036	1054	11 2	1121	1154	1221	1254	1 21	1 51

continued—	p.m.	p.m.	p.m.	p.m.	p.m.	p.m.	p.m.	p.m.	p.m.	p.m.	†	p.m.	p.m.	†	p.m.	p.m.	p.m.
EUSTON..........	1 35	*		2 35	*		*	3 35			X	5 35	†	X		6 10	†
BROAD STREET		1 38	1 45		2 15	2 45	3 15		3 45	4 45	5 5		5 15	5 48	5 45		6 8
LOUDOUN ROAD	**1 44**	**1 56**	**2 14**	**2 44**	**2 49**	**3 14**	**3 37**	**3 44**	**4 14**	**5 14**	**5 23**	**5 44**	**5 49**	**6 6**	**6 14**	**6 19**	**6 29**
KILBURN	1 47	1 59	2 16	2 47	2 52	3 16	3 40	3 47	4 16	5 16	5 26	5 47	5 52	6 8	6 16	6 22	6 31
WILLESDEN	1 54	2 4	2 21	2 54	2 57	3 21	3 44	3 54	4 21	5 21	5 30	5 54	5 57	6 13	6 21	6 28	6 37

continued—	p.m.	p.m.	p.m.	p.m.	p.m.	p.m.	p.m.	p.m.	p.m.	p.m.	p.m.	p.m.	SUNDAYS. a.m.	p.m.	p.m.	p.m.
EUSTON	†	6 35			7 35		8 35		9 35		1035		8 30	2 40	6 45	1015
BROAD STREET	6 15		6 45	7 15		7 45		8 45		9 45		1030				
LOUDOUN ROAD	**6 44**	**6 44**	**7 14**	**7 44**	**7 44**	**8 14**	**8 44**	**9 14**	**9 44**	**1014**	**1044**	**1059**	**8 40**	**2 51**	**6 54**	**1024**
KILBURN	6 46	6 47	7 16	7 46	7 47	8 16	8 47	9 16	9 47	1016	1047	11 1	8 44	2 54	6 57	1027
WILLESDEN	6 51	6 53	7 21	7 51	7 54	8 21	8 54	9 21	9 54	1021	1054	11 6	8 52	3 2	7 5	1033

* Saturdays only. † Not on Saturdays X Express.

A MARBLE CLOCK for 25/6
9 inches high.
Goes 8 days.—Garranted to give satisfaction
WEBSTER,
45, Loudoun Road, N.W.
Opposite Loudoun Rd., Station.

James WAIN & CO.,
FAMILY GROCERS,
Italian Warehousemen, Wine, Spirit, and Bottled Beer Merchants,
45 & 49, FAIRFAX ROAD, ST. JOHN'S WOOD.

Agent for Phillips & Co., Brewers to Her Majesty and Royal Family, Mortlake, S.W.

GEORGE SOLESBURY,
(late W. SHEPHERD & CO.),
Wine, Spirit, Beer, & Mineral Water
MERCHANT,
3, SWISS TER., BELSIZE RD., ST. JOHN'S WOOD.
(Three doors from Swiss Cottage Station.)

A single Bottle of Wine, Spirits, or Beer may be had at wholesale prices.

G. N. ANDREWS,
General Draper & Silk Mercer,
Leicester House,
63, FAIRFAX ROAD,
(Two minutes walk from the Loudoun Road Station & Swiss Cottage.)

USE Hundreds of Testimonials.
Hartstone's Quininé Hairwash
From 1/6 per Bottle.
T. HARTSTONE,
Ladies & Gentlemen's Coiffeur,
67, Fairfax Road, St. John's Wood

ROBERTSON, BROS.
FAMILY BOOT AND SHOE
MANUFACTURERS,
71, Fairfax Road, South Hampstead;
and at 6, St. Margaret's Terrace, Kilburn.

Repairs promptly and neatly executed.

J. M. LAMB,
IRONMONGER, &c.
119, FINCHLEY ROAD.

Best Crystal & Rock Oils at 1/4 per gall.
Best Colza at 4/- per gallon.
Agent to the London & Lancashire Fire Insurance Co.

THOMAS BROWNING.
Brush, Basket, Mat, and Cooperage
WAREHOUSE.

TRUNKS & BOXES IN GREAT VARIETY.

7, Swiss Terrace, Belsize Road.
(Opposite Swiss Cottage Station.)

148. *South Hampstead Advertiser*, front page of first edition, 1880.

TRADES

Forerunner of many a local free-sheet, the *South Hampstead Advertiser* was produced by a printer in Fairfax Road and 'Circulated Gratuitously to every House in the District'. Designed mainly to promote West Hampstead tradesmen, the first edition in December 1880 included such bargain offers as an eight-day marble clock for £1.30. Within ten years circulation had trebled to 6000 weekly, and Baines commented in his *Records of Hampstead*: 'It has met a want of the district, as a considerable proportion of the houses change their tenants every three or four years, who consequently take so little interest in local matters that they will not *purchase* the local paper.' The *Advertiser* grew into the *Hampstead News*, which was a rival to the *Ham and High* until its demise in the 1970s.

The growth of West Hampstead in the railway era changed the face of Kilburn High Road. The small shops in our picture *(149)* – tobacconist, dining rooms, secondhand furniture and bootmaker – had all disappeared by the end of the century and been replaced by more impressive emporia. The North Western Furnishing Company, the Metropolitan

149. Nos. 276–282 Kilburn High Road, c1884.

Boot Company and other chains opened branches in the High Road alongside grandiose buildings for banks, insurance companies and such cultural enterprises as the Kilburn Athenaeum. Dominating the south-west stretch was the long-fronted drapery store of B.B. Evans which, despite a disastrous fire in 1910, flourished here until the 1960s.

Meanwhile, in Belsize Park, the old lane that in the 18th century led to James England's farm had developed into the shopping parade of England's Lane. The elegant terraces on the north side, with an extraordinary number of street lamps, were counterpointed on the south by Wychcombe Studios and a private road, called Chalcot Gardens after an early name for the local farm. Chalcot had changed into Chalk Farm by the 18th century.

Rosslyn Hill had a continuous line of shops from Pilgrims Lane to Willoughby Road until 1898 when the two small buildings above the Rosslyn Arms, on the left of our picture *(153)*, were bought and demolished by the Unitarians. Their new chapel had been built in 1862 and enlarged in 1885, and the congregation now wished to have a more spacious entrance. The other buildings in the picture, including the much-admired Lloyds Bank, a Listed Building by Horace Field in 1896, have hardly changed at all.

150. *B.B. Evans*, Nos. 142–162 Kilburn High Road; the great fire in January 1910.

151. *Cresswell's Dairy* at 71 Kingsgate Road, c1895.

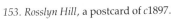
152. *England's Lane*, a turn-of-the-century photograph.

153. *Rosslyn Hill*, a postcard of *c*1897.

OPEN SPACES

To the west of Frognal, Oak Hill Park was developed around 1851 and in that year won a Great Exhibition award for Gentlemen's Dwellings. Redington Road was laid out in 1875, but in the early years only the east end was built, notably a new vicarage for the parish church. Other manorial meadows to the south were appropriated slowly and their streets given mostly Maryon Wilson estate names, such as Bracknell, Chesterford and Lindfield. Greenaway Gardens commemorated the children's artist, who lived in Frognal.

Not surprisingly developers had for some time been casting greedy eyes on two patches of manorial waste in West Hampstead – West End Green and Fortune Green. Since the early 1870s, with the approval of the Manor Court, various builders had attempted to enclose the Greens and had even boarded them up. But local residents, mindful of their age-old tenants' rights and anxious to preserve their recreation grounds, tore the boarding down. West End Green was bought by the Vestry in 1885, but the battle for Fortune Green raged until December 1893 when a band of gypsies, probably encouraged by the frustrated builders, took over part of the Green and chained their caravans to a tree. Two days before Christmas a large crowd of indignant locals rallied and evicted the gypsies, and later pressed the Vestry to buy the land from the Manor. In 1897, after the necessary £8000 had been raised, thanks largely to the LCC and Sir Henry Harben, Fortune Green went public.

154. *Eviction of gypsies from Fortune Green* drawn by Crowther for the *Daily Graphic*, 1893.

155. *Frognal Lane area*, looking towards Kilburn, from a watercolour by Harold Lawes, 1890.

THE BOER WAR

As the records proudly show, Hampstead Volunteers responded readily down the centuries to the nation's calls to arms. The Napoleonic Wars prompted the formation in 1798 of the Loyal Hampstead Association, whose ceremonial drum has fortunately been preserved and can be seen at the Hampstead Museum in Burgh House. Another invasion scare in 1859 brought about the Hampstead Rifle Volunteer Corps, whose drill halls included the old Long Room in Well Walk and the future Everyman Cinema. The only battles they fought were on field days on the Heath, but later Rifle Volunteers, merged into the Territorial Army in 1908, were involved in full-scale wars on foreign soil. A surge of patriotism swept Hampstead during the South African War, culminating in the wild rejoicings in May 1900 at the relief of Mafeking. Our picture *(156)* shows celebrations outside Jack Straw's Castle. According to the *Sphere*, 'there were clowns and pierrot bands, Cameron Highlanders, a file of Bloomsbury Rifles, Church Lads Brigade and so on'. An imitation naval gun, shown in the corner of the picture, had been made especially out of cardboard and canvas and mounted on a handcart.

156. *Hampstead rejoices at the relief of Mafeking*, from the *Sphere*, 26 May 1900.

157. *Reservists march down the High Street* on their way to fight in South Africa, February 1900 (photograph by Arthur Knowles Brown).

Edwardian Enterprise

MANSIONS

At the beginning of the 20th century the stately homes of Hampstead had never had it so good. Kidderpore Hall, built by an East India merchant and named after a district of Calcutta where he had tanneries, was in the safe hands of Westfield College. Hailed as the Girton of North London, the college became part of London University in 1902 (but did not admit male students until 1964).

Bellmoor, at the top of East Heath Road, was the palatial residence of Thomas J. Barratt, already at work on his monumental local history, *The Annals of Hampstead*, published in 1912. Barratt made his fortune from Pears Soap, of which he became chairman in 1865 at the age of 24. In the same year he married Mary Pears, the founder's daughter. Known as 'the father of modern advertising', Barratt earned the title from his innovative promotional ideas, such as buying Millais's painting *Bubbles* and reproducing it with a bar of Pears soap inserted in the corner; he was also responsible for *Pears Cyclopaedia*, first published in 1897.

Another soap magnate, a lifelong friendly rival of Barratt, came to live at The Hill in North End Way, a few hundred yards to the north of Bellmoor, in 1906. This was William Lever, later Lord Leverhulme, who made his millions from Sunlight soap. He bought and beautified The Hill, adding two wings and creating a ballroom, an art gallery, crammed with masterpieces, and a set of rooms designed in different periods. He acquired adjoining properties and was only baulked in his expansion plans by a public right of way behind his grounds. This was another ancient right that Hampstead was not prepared to forfeit. After Leverhulme's death in 1925 the property was bought by Lord Inverforth, who bequeathed it to Manor House Hospital in 1955 *(161 and 162)*.

On a smaller scale, Moreton, on the west side of Holly Walk, was also notable for its art collection. In fact it was designed by Thomas Garner in 1896 for Frederick Sidney, a Fellow of the Society of Antiquaries, who lived there surrounded by his works of art until the 1930s; his initials and crest are over the door *(163)*.

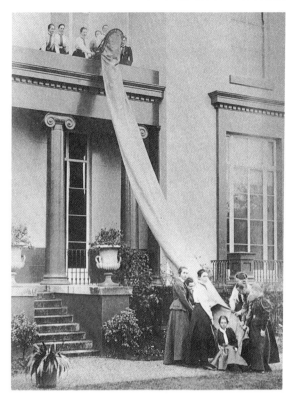

158. *Westfield College* at Kidderpore Hall, fire drill in the early 1900s.

159. *Thomas J. Barratt*, the author of *Annals of Hampstead*.

160. *Bellmoor*, the Moorish room in Barratt's mansion in East Heath Road.

161. *The Hill*, the Stuart room in Leverhulme's house in
North End Way, drawn by T. Raffles Davison.

162. *Viscount Leverhulme*, photographed by Cecil.

163. *(Facing page) Moreton*, Holly Walk, 1910.

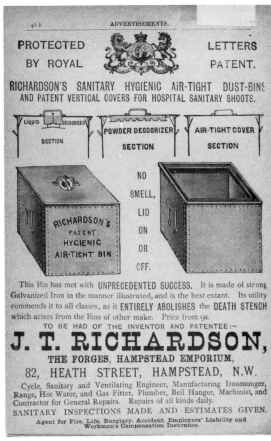

164. Heath Street shops in 1903, photographed before the tube was dug.

165. The Forges, Hampstead Emporium, advertisement in a street directory of 1899.

166. Heath Street, a turn-of-the-century photograph.

HEATH STREET AND HIGH STREET

In 1903 the builders of the Hampstead tube took the wise precaution, before tunnelling began, of photographing all the buildings along the route: they did not want to be accused unfairly of causing cracks in already cracked walls. As a result, a full record of the relevant local frontages has survived to give us a detailed picture of Edwardian Hampstead.

The Heath Street shops in our June 1903 picture *(164)* have all disappeared. From left to right they were Mrs Emerson, butcher, with rabbits hanging outside; John Crowe, undertaker, who later moved to the High Street; Roff & Son, builders; Ferris, bespoke bootmaker; Messenger & Co., builders and decorators; and the Tyne Main Coal Co., offering 'lowest summer prices'. At the same time, higher up the street, the Nag's Head pub had recently been rebuilt (it is now listed 'for curiosity value') and across the road at no. 76 (now a restaurant), Street & Raymond were shown in the directory as cowkeepers. At no. 82 (now a boutique) John Thomas Richardson was called simply ironmonger but, as his advertisement showed, he was offering his services

as a cycle, sanitary and ventilating engineer, gas fitter, bell hanger, insurance agent, etc. etc. But the main attraction of his shop was his patented hygienic dustbin which 'entirely abolishes the death stench'.

At the corner with the High Street half a dozen houses and shops and a cul-de-sac called Minerva Place were demolished by 1907 to make way for the Charing Cross, Euston and Hampstead Railway. Now part of the Northern Line, the Underground Railway to Golders Green was an enormous engineering feat. Tunnelling beneath the Heath was at 250 feet below ground and Hampstead Station is the deepest on the Tube: it made a popular air raid shelter in two World Wars.

One nearby building that escaped disturbance from the Tube was the two-storey superstructure at the entrance to Flask Walk *(168)*, but it all fell down in 1911. A few doors down, Bird in Hand Yard, attached to the pub of that name (now a café), had a similar covered entry, which led to the stables of the London Omnibus Company. In the 19th century, four-horse buses ran regularly from here to the City and Charing Cross, roughly following the routes of

167.'Old houses bought to pull down' at the corner of Heath Street and High Street, c1905.

the present Tube lines. A photograph of *c*1905 *(170)*, shows one of the last of these omnibuses waiting outside the Bird in Hand, together with many other horse-drawn vehicles, all to be superseded shortly by the underground railway and the combustion engine.

Jobmasters (carriage hirers) such as Lansdown Bros. *(171)* seen here outside their premises at nos. 77–78 High Street (now the Hampstead Community Centre), easily converted their businesses to motorised transport, as did livery stables, later offering garage space and engine repairs. Car hire firms were soon thriving. But hordes of people, who relied on horse-minding for their daily bread, found themselves out of work.' 'Ungry and 'opeless', said one of the unemployed, 'and not an 'orse's 'ead to 'old!'

168. *(Facing page) Entrance to Flask Walk* by William Monk, 1901.

169. *Car hire advertisement* in 1921 *Kelly's Directory*.

170. *Hampstead High Street*, looking south, *c*1905.

THE HAMPSTEAD
AND
SWISS COTTAGE MOTOR CO.
LIMITED,

Managing Director: F. WHITEMAN SMITH.

100, Finchley Road and
107 to 109, Avenue Rd.,
LONDON, N.W.3.

LARGEST GARAGE IN N.W. LONDON.
:: GARAGE HOLDS 50 CARS. ::

CARS FOR HIRE.
OPEN DAY and NIGHT.
Telephone : HAMPSTEAD 864.

171. Lansdown Bros., at 77–78 High Street, c1900.

172. Taylor and Lown Ltd, jobmasters, Rosemont Road, c1910.

AND AT
**The West
Hampstead
Livery
Stables,
167,
BROADHURST
GARDENS.**

Telephone
1287
Hampstead.

AND AT
**The Eton
Avenue
Livery
Stables,
ETON AVENUE.**

Telephone
1288
Hampstead.

AND

**HIGHWAY
HOUSE,
CHILD'S HILL,
N.W.**

Telephone
3496 P.O.
Hampstead.

TAYLOR & LOWN Ltd., Motor and Carriage Jobmasters,
Rosemont Road,
FINCHLEY ROAD, N.W.
MOTOR CARS FOR HIRE.
Telephone 683 Paddington

173. Aerial photograph of Whitestone Pond area, c1916.

174. Queen Victoria Rifles, 9th London Regiment, training near Whitestone Pond, 1915.

From War to War

1914–18

An aerial photograph of Hampstead (173) taken about 1916 shows the anti-Zeppelin gun emplacement installed that year beside Whitestone Pond. Otherwise Hampstead seems to be carrying on as usual, paddling in the pond and enjoying the (much-eroded) West Heath. Of general interest are (bottom right) sizeable residences along West Heath Road, with the newly-built Temple Hill House facing the camera and, to the right of it, The Grange. The latter was developed on the site of an ancient house called The Salt Box, seen in many of Constable's local views. Near Judges Walk there is evidence of sand-digging. This dates from the Lord of the Manor's provocative actitivies in the 19th century and is not part of the wartime diggings, when sand was excavated for sandbags.

The Heath was also used as a training ground for London regiments and for combined field exercises. A contingent of the 'Artists' Rifles' frequently marched to the Heath via Fitzjohns Avenue, halting there for a breather, but so many young ladies appeared with cake, wine and cyder that, one of the soldiers recalled, 'the halt became more like a summer garden party'.

175. Rosslyn Lodge Auxiliary Hospital, c1917.

176. Hospital Appeal in the *Ham & High*, April 1917.

177. Tank Day Advertisement in the *Ham & High*, March 1918.

"SPARE WHAT YOU CAN FOR OTHER MEN LIKE ME," and send to The Hampstead War Hospital Supply Depot, 91 Finchley Road, who have hundreds working for the wounded but URGENTLY WANT MONEY to buy materials.

EVERY SHILLING YOU GIVE BUYS something a Wounded Man needs.

SAVE YOUR MONEY FOR

HAMPSTEAD TANK DAY,

Monday, March 4th.

The TANK will await YOU at

FINCHLEY ROAD

(Opposite JOHN BARNES & CO.),

Near FINCHLEY RD., METROPOLITAN STATION.

Hours 10 a.m. till 9 p.m.,

AND WILL SELL WAR BONDS,

£5 to £5000, and

WAR SAVING CERTIFICATES,

15s. 6d.

178. Fund-raising tank outside Finchley Road Station, March 1918.

Several large houses were requisitioned as hospitals or convalescent homes, including Rosslyn Lodge in Lyndhurst Road, Cedar Lawn in North End Way, part of Lord Leverhulme's estate, and Kenwood House. The latter was made available by its current tenant, Grand Duke Michael of Russia. Equipment and materials for hospitals at home and abroad were provided by the Hampstead War Hospital Supply Depot at no. 91 Finchley Road. Voluntary workers gathered in groups to make bandages, bedjackets, crutches, splints and pyjamas. Flag Days and other fund-raising, such as Tank Days, were all part of the home front's campaign to 'Back your sailors and soldiers with your money'. On Hampstead's Tank Day in 1918, seen in our picture *(178)*, civic dignitaries, including the Mayor and his mace-bearer, were joined by the actor-manager Gerald du Maurier (second from right), who lived at Cannon Hall.

179. *John Barnes Great White Sale* in March 1917 greets the 'dawn of coming victory' with undoubted bargains.

WRITERS BETWEEN THE WARS

In August 1918, the month before the war ended, the New Zealand writer, Katherine Mansfield, came to live in East Heath Road. Newly married to the critic, John Middleton Murry, she chose Hampstead in the hope that its healthy air would cure her tuberculosis, but she was also one of a circle of distinguished writers who frequented the area over a number of years. D.H. Lawrence had his only London home in the Vale of Health; Lytton Strachey lived in Belsize Park Gardens, where he completed his *Eminent Victorians*, Aldous Huxley had a flat in Hampstead Hill Gardens, and Leonard and Virginia Woolf were constant visitors.

Outside their circle, John Galsworthy, who also arrived in 1918, chose a modest house, Grove Lodge, next to Admiral's House. He was at the height of his fame and during his days in Hampstead completed his masterpiece, *The Forsyte Saga*. By 1932, when he was honoured with the Nobel Prize for Literature, he had become an invalid and was unable to collect his award. However, a delegation delivered the prize to Grove Lodge in 1933, a short time before his death.

J.B. Priestley also came to Hampstead in his years of fame, living in Well Walk soon after the success of his novel *The Good Companions* in 1929. George Orwell, on the other hand, badly needed a job and became a bookshop assistant in Pond Street in 1934–5. His reactions to Hampstead are reflected in his *Keep the Aspidistra Flying*.

180. *Katherine Mansfield* lived at 17 East Heath Road, which she called 'The Elephant'.

181. *John Galsworthy* at Grove Lodge.

182. *Tank appeal* in the High Street during World War II.

1939–45

Tank Days and Savings Drives returned to Hampstead in World War II, with a special appeal to support the sailors on HMS Hampstead. The bombing of London did not begin until September 1940, and the first high explosives to fall on Hampstead that month destroyed houses in Upper Park Road, Parkhill Road and Downside Crescent. The sirens continued to sound on succeeding nights, and the gravity of the incidents increased. On one night a stick of bombs fell in the Mill Lane area, causing widespread damage in Sumatra Road, and killing nineteen people. Later, a number of other areas, such as New End Square, were nearly obliterated by night bombers. According to the official report in *Hampstead At War*, a total of 467 missiles and thousands of incendiary bombs hit the borough, causing 1,134 casualties and damaging over 13,500 houses.

183. New End Square after bombing, with blast shelter (centre) and Emergency Water Supply (left).

184. Swiss Cottage tube shelterers in a mixed dormitory.

185. The Central Library in Arkwright Road, hit by a rocket, 1945.

After a brief ban on using tube stations, residents flocked to take shelter in them, and sometimes formed themselves into social groups. Regular shelterers at Swiss Cottage station even produced their own bulletin, *The Swiss Cottager*, organised entertainments and refreshments and campaigned for better facilities. Among other problems, they protested at having to take a train to Finchley Road Station to find a proper toilet.

The last major incident in Hampstead's war was caused by a V2 rocket landing near the Central Library (now Camden Arts Centre) in Arkwright Road in the last weeks of the war. Over eight hundred houses were damaged, but only fourteen people were injured and nobody was killed. 'As the shadow of war moved from this corner of north-west London,' concluded *Hampstead at War*, 'there came the end of 2,155 nights of blackout, when mothers could put their children to bed with the feeling that they would be safe and sound in the morning.'

The Coming of Camden

HOUSING

Wartime bombing created many suitable sites for new housing, which were quickly acquired but only slowly developed by both private and public organisations. One of the first major post-war projects of the Hampstead Borough Council was the building of the Wells House blocks of flats in Well Walk, designed to harmonise with the Queen Anne style of Burgh House; they were awarded a RIBA Bronze Medal in 1949. More council houses came to Broadhurst Gardens which had, along with other West Hampstead areas bordering the railways, suffered badly in the bombing. Adelaide Road was given an entirely new image; Constable House was one of the first large blocks built here in the 1950s, but

186. Adelaide Road with incipient tower block, June 1967.

187. *Fleet Road* being redeveloped in 1963.

188. *Flask Walk*, south side, 1960s.

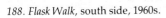

it was dwarfed by the 23-storey towers which followed from 1965. Being on the old Eton Estate, the high-rise blocks called Dorney, Bray, Taplow and Burnham were named from villages near Eton. Terraces in Fleet Road were also demolished and replaced by council flats, with names commemorating three Hampstead residents – Sir Francis Palgrave, Robert Stephenson and Sarah Siddons.

Higher up the hill, old buildings in Flask Walk, including a grocer, a Salvation Army hall and a Montessori school, were completely and ingeniously redeveloped by private enterprise.

SHOPPING

On the north side of Flask Walk most of the early 19th century workers' cottages have survived, and so have the old shops at the High Street end. However, the chemist and greengrocer in the picture *(189)* and the fishmongery which had operated (with or without chips) from the 1860s, are now long gone.

So are many other small and useful shops that served the community of central Hampstead. In the High Street Fowler's at no. 40 had been in the same line of business since the 1850s when the proprietor was called an oil and colourman. Oil jars, seen above his shopfront, were his trade signs. The premises, including the Bird in Hand pub next door, were rebuilt in the 1870s and the business was expanded into general ironmongery, but in 1979 commercial considerations pushed out Fowler's and brought in a boutique. Fortunately, the oil jars were salvaged for the Hampstead Museum. Below the Bird in Hand the ancient Norway Yard was redeveloped in the 1930s as the Blue Star Garage. The protests at the time were about as vociferous as the outcry in the 1980s when the garage was supplanted by superior shops and luxury housing.

189. Flask Walk, Nos. 1–7 in 1943.

190. High Street, Nos. 39 and 40, before change of use.

Round the corner in Heath Street, a Georgian terrace had already been demolished for a new shopping precinct, designed by Ted Levy Benjamin & Partners, and christened Kingswell. The whole pattern of local shopping changed from the 1970s as higher rents forced out old-established businesses and introduced the sort of shops that appealed more to visitors than to residents. Sadly, most of the shops are controlled by large companies based many miles away, who appear not at all interested in the welfare of the local community they serve. The same problem applies to the three dozen or so restaurants in the area, which are too highly priced for the average inhabitant, and to the ever-increasing numbers of estate agents' offices, selling houses, which few in Hampstead can afford.

CAMDEN

Hampstead's biggest redevelopment since the war has been at the Town Hall. One of the old Borough Council's last major achievements, as part of the projected Civic Centre at Swiss Cottage, was the completion of the swimming pool and library, designed by Sir Basil Spence. These were opened by the Queen in 1964. In the following year, along with Holborn and St Pancras, Hampstead was absorbed into the new London Borough of Camden. The Mayor of Hampstead laid down his chain of office, the old Town Hall on Haverstock Hill was taken over by Camden Works Department and Hampstead, as defined by the thousand-year-old boundaries, ceased to exist.

But all is not lost. Records of the past are well preserved in Camden's Local History Library at Swiss Cottage, and in the Hampstead Museum at Burgh House where, among many reminders of Hampstead's illustrious history, the mayoral chair has pride of place.

191. Heath Street houses (1941), on the site of Kingswell (1972).

192. *Swiss Cottage Library*, opened by the Queen, 1964.

193. *The penultimate Mayor and Mayoress of Hampstead*, Councillor and Mrs Oatway (left), at a Civic Reception in Hampstead Town Hall, with the Rt. Hon. Henry Brooke, MP for Hampstead, and Dame Barbara Brooke, February 1964.

194. *The Great Flood* of 14 August 1975, photographed by the *Ham & High*.

Index

Illustrations are indicated in bold
type

ABERNETHY HOUSE, 66
Adelaide Tavern, 36, **36**
Adelaide Road, 36, 137, **137**
Admiral's House, 29, 71, **71**, 72
All Souls, Loudon Road, 98
America, 12, 14, 39, 59
Antrim Road library, 108, **108**
Armada 12
Artists in Hampstead, 71–75
Artists' Rifles, 129
Athenaeum, Vale of Health, 84, **85**
Avenue Road, 63
Ayrton, Maxwell, 110

BAMBRIDGE, Capt George and Elsie, 18
Baptists' Chapel, 66–67, **67**, 100
Barbauld, Mrs, 41
Barratt, Thomas J., 16, 38, 120, **120**
Bartram House, 90, **90**
Beating the Bounds, 54, **54**
Beaton, Sir Cecil, 36
Beckford family, 54
Bell, Kilburn, 23, **23**
Bellmoor, 38, 120, **121**
Belsize farmhhouse, 12, **13**, 91
Belsize House, 12, 23–24, **24**, 52
Belsize Lane, 12, 29, 97
Belsize Tunnel, 76, 98
Binning, Lady, 18
Bird in Hand, 125, 127, **139**
Black Lion, 32
Blake, William, 11
Blomfield, Sir Arthur, 32
Blue Star Garage, 139
Boer War, 119, **119**
Bonfire on Heath, 84, **85**
Boys' Home, **91**
Brabazon, Sir Roger le, 12
Bradley's Buildings, 94, **96**
Branch Hill Lodge, 14, 45, **45**
Branch Hill Pond **9**
Brent river, 9
Broadhurst Gardens, 137
Brook, Clive, 47, **51**
Brooke, Rt. Hon. Henry, **141**
Broomsleigh Street, 100
Brown, Ford Madox, 72, **72**
Buckingham, Duke of, 14
Budden, W.H., 65
Bull and Bush, 39, 51, 69, **69**
Burgh House, 18, **19**, **25**, 28, 29, 86, **87**
Burgh, Rev. Allatson, 18
Burney, Fanny, 27, **27**, 28
Buses 125, 127
Butler, Bishop, 16
Butler, J.D., 105
Byron, Lady, 39, 45
Byron Cottage, 39

CAMDEN COUNCIL, 18, 46, 68, 140

Camden History Society, 43
Campden family, 68, 104
Cannon Hall and Lane, 47, 105, 131
Carlile House estate 89
Carline family, 58
Chalcot Gardens, 116
Chalk Farm, 11
Chatelain, J.B., 25
Chesterfield, Earls of, 23, 43
Chestnut Lodge, 47
Chicken House, Rosslyn Hill, 12–13, **13**, **14**, 14
Cholmley Lodge, 54
Christ Church, 22, 38, 82, 97, 100
Christian Science Church, 46
Church Place, 94, **94**
Church Row, 22, 40–41, **40**, **41**, 52
City Arms, 112, **113**
Clarke, Sir Thomas, 45
Cock and Hoop, 54
College Crescent, 62
Congregational Church, Lyndhurst Road, 98, **99**
Constable, John, 32, 43, 58, 71–72, **71**, 108
Cresswell's Dairy, **116**
Crossfield Road, 100, 103
Crowe, John, 125
Cruchley's map, **60**, 61
Crump, Miss, 76

DANBY, THOMAS, 75
Defoe, Daniel, 22
De Gaulle, General, 52
Dickens, Charles, 11, 46, 69
Domesday Survey of Hampstead 8
Donkeys at Hampstead, 79, **79**
Douglas, Lord Alfred, 41
Downshire Hill, 57–58, **57**
du Maurier, Daphne, 47, **47**
du Maurier, George, 41, 43, 69, 79, **79**
du Maurier, Sir Gerald, 36, 43, 47, **47**, 131
Duffield, John 20, 22
Duval, Claude, 51

EBENEZER STRICT BAPTIST CHAPEL, 67
Electricity supply, 109, **109**
Ellerdale Road, 66
Elizabeth I, 12
Elm Row, 22
Emmanuel School, 54, **55**, 57
Emmanuel Church, West End Green, 98
Engels, F., 69
England's Lane, 110, 116, **117**
Erith, Raymond, 69
Eton College Estate, 11, 139
Evans, B.B., 116, **116**
Evelyn, John, 12
Everyman Cinema, 94, 119
Eyre, Colonel, 61

FENTON HOUSE, 18, **18**
Field, Edwin, 47
Field, Horace, 46, 47, 116
Fiennes Celia, 20
Finchley Road, 61–63, 131
Finchley Road Station 76, **76**
Fire services, 106, **106**, **107**
First World War – see World Wars
Fitzjohns Avenue, 61, 92, 94

Fitzjohns Primary School, **44**
Flagstaff, Whitestone Pond, 12, **12**
Flask Tavern, 20
Flask Walk, 20, 80, 105, 108, 125, **126**, **138–139**, 139
Flask Walk Baths, 68
Fleet river, 9–10, 59, 83, 100
Fleet Road, **138**
Fleet Road School, 100, **100**
Flitcroft, Henry, 45
Flooding in Hampstead, **141**
Forde, Florrie, 69
Fortune Green, 110, 118, **118**
Fowler's, 139, **139**
Freud, E.L., 73
Frognal, 26, 27, **27**, 48, 52
Frognal Close, 73
Frognal Gardens, 41
Frognal Hall, **42**
Frognal Lane, 52, **118**
Frognal Priory (new), 73, **74**
Frognal Priory (old), 73, **73**

GAINSBOROUGH family, 20, **21**, 104
Gainsborough, Thomas, 69, 71
Gainsborough Gardens, 20, 22
Gaitskell, Hugh, 43
Galsworthy, John, 72, 133, **133**
Garner, Thomas, 120
Gay, John, 22
Gee, Joshua, 18
George Inn, 106
Gerard, John, 39
Gibberd, Sir Frederick, 58
Gibbet Elms, 51, **47**
Gibbons, Dr., 18
Goldsmith, Oliver, 26
Gordon Riots, 44, 69
Gospel Oak, 54
Grange, The, Kilburn High Road, **56**, 57
Grange Park, 57
Green, T.K., 75
Greenaway, Kate, 73, 118
Grove Lodge, 133
Gypsies, 118, **118**

HABERDASHERS' Aske's School, **102**, 103
Hall Oak Farm, 52
Hall School, 100, **102**, 103
Hampstead
   coat of arms, 104, **104**
   Domesday Survey, 8
   early charter, 10
   incorporation into Camden, 104, 140
   incorporation into London, 104
   Hampstead and Highgate Express, 36, 67, 115
Hampstead Central Library, Arkwright Road, 108, 136, **136**
Hampstead Central Library, Swiss Cottage, 140, **141**
Hampstead Community Centre, 36, 127
Hampstead Comprehensive School, 103
Hampstead Dispensary, 86, 112
Hampstead Garden Suburb, 11
Hampstead General Hospital, 90
Hampstead Heath, 8–10, **8**, **9**, 38–39, 129
   brickmaking on 92, **93**
   building on **88**, 89
   digging on, 89, **89**, 129
   holiday crowds 76–84, **82**

Hampstead Heath Station, 59, 76, **78**, 79
Hampstead High Street, 29, 34, **35**, 36, 96, **96, 97**, 107, 125, **125–128, 139**
Hampstead is the place to ruralise, **81**
Hampstead Museum, 18, 119, 139, 140
Hampstead News, 115
Hampstead Parish Church, 10, **10, 42,** 43, 72
Hampstead Parochial Schools, 66, **67,** 94, 100
Hampstead Ponds, 11, 59, 79, **80**
Hampstead Rifle Volunteer Corps, 119
Hampstead Spa, see Hampstead Wells
Hampstead Subscription Library, 46, 108
Hampstead Underground station, 125
Hampstead Vestry 48, 96, 104
Hampstead Volunteers, 22
Hampstead Water Company, 59
Hampstead Wells, 17, 20–22, 25–28, **25, 26, 28**
  1st Long Room, 20, **20,** 22, **22,** 98, 119
  2nd Long Room, 25, **25, 28**
Hampstead Wells Trust or Charity, 20, 67–68
Harben, Sir Henry, 104, **104,** 118
Hardy, Thomas 32
Hare and Hounds, 39
Harrison, John, 43
Haverstock Hill, 32, **33,** 49, 75, 100, 104
Heath Lodge, North End, 52
 Heath Mount, **37**
Heath Mount School, 36
Heath Street, 22, 29, 36, **37,** 66, **72,** 96, **124, 125,** 125, **140**
Henry VIII, 11, 12
Hepworth, Barbara, 75
Highwaymen, 51
Hill, Sir Rowland, 90, **90**
Hill, The, 52, 120, 122
Hoare, John Gurney, 89
Hogarth, William, 69, 71
Holl, Frank, 92
Holland, Sir Henry, 104
Hollow Elm, 16–17, **16**
Holly Bush Hill, 71
Holly Bush Vale, 66, 68, 94
Holly Hill, 29, 105
Holly Mount, 67
Holly Place and Walk, **52,** 105, 120
Hopkins, Michael, 58
Houston, Lady, 39
Howell, 23
Hunt, Leigh, 58, 83
Huxley, Aldous, 133

INVERFORTH, Lord, 120
Irving, Washington, 32, 69

JACK STRAW'S CASTLE, 48, 51, 69, **70**
Jackson, Francis, 51
James I, 12, 14
Jekyll, Gertrude, 18
Joad, Cyril, 43
Jobmasters, 127
John Barnes, **132]*]**
Johnson, Dr Samuel, 26, 28
Judges Walk, 17, 17, 29

KEATS, JOHN, 43, 58–59, **58,** 83
Keats Grove, 58
Keats House, 58–59, **58**
Kenwood House, 69, 131

Key family, 46
Keynes, Sir Geoffrey, 49
Kidderpore Hall, 120
Kilburn High Road, 11, 32, **34, 33,** 115, **115**
Kilburn Priory 10–11, **10,** 23, 54
Kilburn Wells, 23, 32
King, C.B., 41
King of Bohemia, 14, **15**
King's Well, 34
Kingswell, 34, 140, **140**
Kipling, Rudyard, 18
Kit-Cat Club, 22, 32
Kneller, Godfrey, 22
Knox E.V., 43
Kyngeswell, Robert de, 34

LAMB, Henry, 84
Lancaster Grove, 106
Lansdown Bros., 127, **128**
Lauriston Lodge, West End, **56,** 57
Lavie, Germain, 57
Lawrence, D.H., 84, 133
Lessingham, Mrs, 52
Leverhulme, Lord, 52, 120, **122**
Libraries, 108, **108**
Linnell, John, 11
Lithos Road, 109
Little Church Row, 94, **95**
Lloyds Bank, 116
Load of Hay, 32
London and Birmingham Railway, 65, **65,** 76
London and North Western Railway, 65, 76
Lower Terrace, 71
Loyal Hampstead Association, 28, 119
Lynd, Robert and Sylvia, 58

MACKENZIE, COMPTON, 84
Mall Studios, 75
Manor Farm, 52, 54
Manor House Hospital, 120
Mansfield, Katherine, 133, **133**
Mansfield, Lord, 14
Maps, **30–31, 53, 60, 86, 88**
Marx, Karl, 69
Maryon Wilson family, 89, 92, 118
Medical Officer of Health, 110
Methodists, 94, 98
Miles family, 54
Milestones, 38
Mill Lane, 29, 57
Milligan, Robert, 44
Mission church, Belsize Lane, 97–98, **97**
Mitchell, Thomas, 66
Moore, Henry, 75
Moreland Hall, 66
Moreton, Holly Walk, 120, **123**
Mount, The, 72, **72**
Mount Vernon Hospital, 46, 110, **111**
Muir, Edwin, 58

NAG'S HEAD, 125
National Institute for Medical Research, 110
National Trust, 18, 47
Neave, Sir Thomas, 14
Netherwood Street, 100
Nevinson, C.R.W., 75
New Campden Court, 68

New College, 62–63
New End, **113**
New End Hospital, 48, 49, **50**
New End School, 100, **101,** 112
New End Square, **135**
New River Company, 59
Nicholson, Ben, 75
North End, 11, 29, 38–39, **38,** 51, 69
North End Place, 39, **39**
North End Way, 38, 131
North London Line, 76, **76, 77,** 78
North Western Fever Hospital, 90, 100
Norway Yard, 139

OAK HILL PARK, 118
Oatway, Norman, **141**
Old Black Lion, 112, **112**
Old Mansion, Frognal, 41
Olde White Bear, 112, **113**
Ordnance Survey of Hampstead, 86, **86**
Oriel House, 94
Orwell, George, 133

PALGRAVE, Sir Francis, 17
Park, John James, 52
Park, Thomas, 52
Parker, Sir Thomas, 45
Parkhill Studios, 75, **75**
Pavlova, Anna, 39
Pearcey, Mrs, 103
Penrose, Sir Roland, 58
Pepys, Samuel, 12
Perceval, Spencer, 24
Pevsner, Sir Nikolaus, 39
Philo-Investigists, 66, **66**
Pitt House, see north End Place
Pitt, William the elder, 39
Platt's Lane, 51
Police 105, **105**
Pond Street, 29, **29,** 34, **32,** 133
Poorhouses, 48, **50**
Pope, Alexander, 26
Povey, Charles, 23
Presbyterians, 22, 98
Priestley, J.B., 133
Primrose Hill Tunnel, 65, **65**
Prince Arthur Road, 46
Priory Lodge, 26–27, **27**
Priory Road, 108

QUEEN VICTORIA RIFLES, 129
Quex Road, 98

RACKHAM, Arthur, 75
Randall's, **110**
Red Lion, Kilburn, 32
Red Lion Hill, 34
Redington road, 118
Richardson, J.T., **124,** 125
Robson, Flora, 58
Rocque map of Hampstead area, 29, **30–31,** 32
Roman Catholics, 98
Romney, George, 71
Rosemont Road, **128**
Rossetti, Dante Gabriel, 58
Rosslyn Chapel, 17, 116
Rosslyn Hill, 12, 34, **34,** 105, **105,** 116, **117**
Rosslyn House, 12, 43–46, **43,** 52
Rosslyn Lodge, **130**
Royal East Middlesex Militia, 18, **86**

Royal Free Hospital, 90
Royal Soldiers' Daughters Home, 16, 44–45, **44**

ST ANDREW, Frognal Lane, 98
St Cuthbert, Fordwych Road, 98
St James, West End Lane, 98
St John, Downshire Hill, 57–58
St John at Hampstead, see Hampstead Parish Church
St Luke, Kidderpore Avenue, 98
St Mary, Abbey Road, 11, 97
St Mary, Holly Place, 52, **52**
St Mary the Virgin, Primrose Hill, 98
St Peter, Belsize Park, 97,
St Saviour, Eton Road, 97
St Stephen, Rosslyn Hill, 98, **99**
Salvation Army, 84
Sanderson, John, 43
Sandy Heath, 38
School for the Blind, 63
Schools in Hampstead, 66, 100
Scott, Sir George Gilbert, 72
Second World War, see World Wars
Sharpe, Henry, 97
Shaw, Norman, 66, 73, 92
Shelford Lodge, 44
Shelley, Percy Bysshe, 83
Shepherd's Well, 9 **9**, 54, 61
Sidney, Frederick, 120
Sion Chapel, 23
Sir Richard Steele pub, 32
Slaughterhouses, 110, **110**
Smith, Roger, 110
Soame, Dr John, 26
South End, 57–59
South End Green, 59, **59**, 80
South End Green fountain, 76
South Hampstead Advertiser, **114**, 115
South Hampstead High School, 100, **101**, 103
Spaniards Inn, 51, 69, **70**
Spence, Sir Basil, 140
Spencer, Stanley, 58, 84, **84**
Squire, Joshua, 47
Squire's Mount, 47, **47**
Stanfield, Clarkson, 46
Stanfield House, 46, **46**, 108
Steele's Cottage, Haverstock Hill, 32, **33**
Steele's Studios, 32, 75
Stoll, Sir Oswald, 57
Strachey, Lytton, 133
Swiss Cottage, 61–63, **62–63**, 140
Swiss Cottage Motor Co., **127**
Swiss Cottage pub, 61, **61, 64**
Swiss Cottage Station, 62, **136**

TASKER ROAD, 75
Tate, Edwin, 73
Ted Levy Benjamin & Partners, 140
Telegraph Hill, 52
Teulon, Samuel Sanders, 45, 98, **98**
Thompson, John, 73
Three Gables, Fitzjohns Avenue, 92, **92**
Three Horseshoes, 96
Tollgates, 12, **32, 41**, 61, 62, 69
Town Hall, 49, 104, 140
Town Improvements, 94–96
Tree, Beerbohm, 43
Treherne House, 57
Trinity Church, Willoughby Road, 98, **98**

Turnpike roads, 32
Turpin, Dick, 51, 57, 69
Tyburn river, 9, 54

UNDERGROUND RAILWAYS, 46, 62, 76, 125
Unitarians, 17, 98, 100, 116
University College School, 103, **103**
Unwin, Sir Raymond, 11
Upper Flask Tavern, 22

VALE OF HEALTH, 17, 48, **50**, 79, 80, 82, 83
Vale of Health Hotel, 83–84, **83**
Vane, Sir Henry, 14, **14**, 16, 45
Vane House, 14, **15**, 45
Viaduct bridge, 89, 92
Victoria, Queen, 12, 44
Villas on the Heath, 83

WAAD, ARMIGAL, 12
Waad, William 12, **12**
Walker, Thomas, 45
Wallace, Edgar, 84
Washerwomen 10, 11, 83, 89
Waterhouse, Alfred, 98
Waugh, Evelyn, 36
Wedderburn, Alexander, 34, 44, **44**, 45
Wedgwood dinner service, 25, **25**
Well Walk, 9, 22, 25, 43, 58, 72, 119, 137
Wells, H.G., 41
Wells and Campden Trust, 68
Wells Court, 67–68, **68**
Wells House, Well Walk, 28, 137
West End, 54–57, **55**, 76
West End Fair, 57
West End Green, 54, 118
West End Hall, 54, **55**
West End House, 54
West End Lane, 29
West Heath Road, 129
Westbourne river, 9
Westfield College, 120, **120**
Westminster Abbey, 10, 11, 12, 34, 104
Whitestone Pond, 12, 36, **37**, 38, 79, **79**
Wildwood Corner, 39
William IV public house, 36
Williamson, Dr George, 18
Willoughby Road, 22, 89, 98
Willow Hall, 86, **87**
Willow Road, 25
Windmills, 8, **8**, 29
Woods, William 58
Woolf, Virginia, 133
Workhouses, 48–49, **48, 49**, 86
World Wars, 129–136, **129–132, 134–136**
Wotton, Lord, 12, 23
Wychcombe Studios, 75, 116
Wyldes 11, **11**, 39

YORKSHIRE GREY YARD and inn, 94